Better Homes & Gardens.

FAST *or* SLOW

Delicious meals for slow cookers, pressure cookers, or multicookers

HOUGHTON MIFFLIN HARCOURT

BOSTON · NEW YORK · 2018

BETTER HOMES & GARDENS® FAST OR SLOW

Contributing Editor: Tricia Bergman

Contributing Copy Editor and Proofreader: Peg Smith, Carrie Truesdell

Test Kitchen Director: Lynn Blanchard

Test Kitchen Product Supervisor: Colleen Weeden

Test Kitchen Home Economists: Sarah Brekke, Linda Brewer, Carla Christian, Juli Hale, Sammy Mila

Contributing Photographers: Jason Donnelly, Jacob Fox, Andy Lyons, Blaine Moats

Contributing Stylists: Kelsey Bulat, Greg Luna, Dianna Nolin

BETTER HOMES & GARDENS®

Editor in Chief: Stephen Orr

Creative Director: Jennifer D. Madara

Executive Food Editor: Jan Miller

Design Director: Stephanie Hunter

HOUGHTON MIFFLIN HARCOURT

Executive Editor: Anne Ficklen

Managing Editor: Marina Padakis Lowry

Art Director: Tai Blanche

Production Director: Tom Hyland

WATERBURY PUBLICATIONS, INC.

Design Director: Ken Carlson

Editorial Director: Lisa Kingsley

Associate Design Director: Doug Samuelson

Our seal assures you that every recipe in *Better Homes & Gardens· Fast or Slow* has been tested in the Better Homes and Gardens® Test Kitchen. This means that each recipe is practical and reliable and meets our high standards of taste appeal. We guarantee your satisfaction with this book for as long as you own it.

Pictured on front cover:
Beer-Soaked Brisket Sandwiches, page 134

Pictured on back cover:
Chicken Shawarma, page 103

CONTENTS

INTRODUCTION

What makes cooking on a Tuesday night different than cooking on the weekend? Time. Time to plan, time to prep and cook. Enter two time-saving appliances. One you know well—the slow cooker—requires time to prep and cook. The other—the pressure cooker—requires prep but cuts cooking time significantly. The recipes in this book offer the option of cooking the same dish in either a slow cooker or pressure cooker with equally delicious results. And you have the choice of how you use your time.

The recipes in *Better Homes & Gardens® Fast or Slow* have been thoroughly tested in our Test Kitchen for both cooking methods and in a variety of types of slow cookers and pressure cookers—both stove-top and electric. There's no more trying to convert your favorite slow cooker recipes to a pressure cooker or vice versa; it's all here in clear, no-fail instructions.

First, a caveat: Be sure to thoroughly read manuals for your specific appliances, because function can vary among brands and types of cooker. Electric pressure cooker and multicooker (such as the Instant Pot®) recipes in this book were tested on high pressure (not using preset buttons). Always bring the pressure cooker up to heat and release pressure—natural or quick release—according to recipe instructions.

In addition to the full instructions for both the slow cooker and pressure cooker, you'll find bonus features scattered throughout the book.

"Up the Flavor" tips offer ideas to enhance or switch the flavor of a recipe (more options!). Information about ingredients, make-ahead tips, and substitutions make recipes even more convenient.

Additionally, many of the recipes in this book have icons at the top to indicate features to consider when meal planning. Here's what each icon represents:

[**WEEKNIGHT**]

These slow cooker recipes can be started in the morning, then it's hands off for 8-plus hours.

[**VEGETARIAN**]

No ingredients contain meat or meat products.

[**HEALTHY**]

Main-dish recipes
Calories: 425 or fewer
Fat: 15 grams or fewer
Protein: 10 grams or more
Fiber: 3 grams or more
Sodium: 800 milligrams or fewer
Sides and snacks
Calories: 175 or fewer
Fat: 8 grams or fewer
Fiber: 1 gram or more
Sodium: 500 milligrams or fewer

[**COMPANY**]

While every recipe is delicious, some are especially company-worthy.

LINGO:
KNOW THE PIECES AND PARTS OF A PRESSURE COOKER

Gasket

Pressure Valve

Programmable Settings

Removable Pot Liner

Mini Chocolate-Orange
Lava Cakes (p 289)

PRESSURE COOKING 101

How does it work? When food cooks, it produces steam. Pressure cookers have an airtight seal (the gasket under the lid) to trap steam and create intense pressure (therefore higher heat) in the cooker. These conditions cook food more quickly and evenly than any other method and yield moist, tender meals—desserts, too!

ELECTRIC

Electric models look like slow cookers (and often have that function as well). Once you read the directions, they are easy to set—just press a button or two. It requires no further supervision; timers track how long it takes the cooker to get up to pressure, cook the food, and depressurize.

EASE OF USE
Overall, these are easy and convenient to use.

VERSATILITY
Most cookers have multiple settings, such as brown, pressure-cook, slow-cook, rice, keep warm, and more.

PRICE
Around $100; higher or lower depending on brand and features of the model.

USING AN ELECTRIC PRESSURE COOKER

All models differ in appearance, parts, and instructions (read your user's manual before you start!). Here's the gist of pressure cooking.

Browning = Flavor

---

1. CHECK IT OFF
Take a quick look at all the parts of your pressure cooker. Make sure the gasket is soft, flexible, and crack-free. Snap it into place as directed in the manual. Make sure the pressure valve is free of debris and in place.

---

2. BROWNING = FLAVOR
Most models have a browning or sauteing function, which is essential if you want meat to have rich, caramelized flavor. Add oil, set the saute function, and allow the pot to heat. Large amounts of cubed or ground meat should be browned in batches to prevent the pot from cooling and steaming the meat instead of browning it.

Set the Pressure

---

3. SET THE PRESSURE
Once the meat is browned, add remaining ingredients as directed in your recipe. Lock the lid into place and adjust the pressure valve to closed or pressure position. Select high-pressure setting and time. The digital display will indicate when the cooker is up to pressure (usually 15 to 20 minutes) and actual cooking time has started to count down.

---

4. LETTING OFF STEAM
Each recipe provides directions for natural or quick release of pressure. When cooking time is done, the cooker will automatically begin to depressurize, which is called "natural release." This generally takes about 15 minutes (quick release happens when you open the pressure valve and let steam rush out—which isn't recommended for liquid recipes, such as soup). When pressure has dropped, the pressure indicator will sink and you will be able to open the lid. (Until then, the lid stays locked.) After 15 minutes of depressurizing, if the lid is still locked, often the pressure valve can be opened to let out remaining steam. The steam will be hot, so use a towel or oven mitt to turn the handle, then step back.

Letting off Steam

---

5. OPEN WITH CAUTION
The food inside is extremely hot, so steam will escape when the lid is opened. Be careful to avoid burning arms and face.

Open with Caution

STOVE TOP

A stove-top pressure cooker looks like a large saucepan and has a lid that locks on tight for safety. It heats up on the stove burner, then requires a bit of monitoring to make sure the heat (and therefore the steam) stays at the right pressure during the cooking process.

EASE OF USE
Stove-top models are slightly less expensive but will need more supervision than electric.

VERSATILITY
It performs browning and pressure-cooking, and it can double as a regular stove-top pan.

PRICE
A more affordable option in the $35 to $100 range.

Pressure indicator

USING A STOVE-TOP PRESSURE COOKER

After browning the meat, adding the remaining ingredients, and locking the lid in place, set the pressure valve per the user's manual. Bring the cooker up to pressure over medium-high heat (you'll know when steam comes out of the valve). Reduce the heat to maintain steady pressure (which will keep the pressure indicator up) for the full cooking time. Remove the cooker from the stove and follow recipe instructions to let the pressure come down naturally (watch for the pressure indicator to drop) or quickly release the pressure.

SLOW COOKER **KNOW-HOW**

When it comes to heating elements, all slow cookers are not created equally, which means that some recipes have varying results. We came face-to-face with differences during thorough testing of the recipes in this book. Here's what we learned:

1. HOW IT WORKS

Coils indirectly transfer heat to the inner crock of the slow cooker. Steam builds in the cooker, and juices that normally release from ingredients—especially meat—during cooking are held in the cooker. The result? Moist, tender meat and veggies without added fat and calories. This top-selling appliance boasts a level of confidence and convenience that no other cooking method can match: the beauty of combining ingredients in the morning, switching it on, and coming home to dinner that is ready to serve.

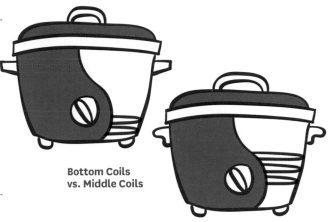

**Bottom Coils
vs. Middle Coils**

2. THE HALF-FULL RULE

Normally we recommend filling a slow cooker at least half full for optimum cooking. However, once we stretched recipe development past pot roast and chili, the old rule came into question. Slow cookers are programmed to gradually heat to a set temperature, regardless how much food is in the crock. Therefore, when we tested baking-type recipes and other recipes that were shallow in the crock, we experienced success with some brands and burning with others.

3. ELEMENT-ARY

To get to the bottom of the issue, we took a couple of paths. We placed calls to the big brands in the market, and we deconstructed several slow cooker models to see how they were built. We learned that some brands run heating elements around the middle of the slow cooker (illustration, right), which allows for even heat distribution even when the load is below the level of the heating element. Other brands have elements closer to the base of the unit (illustration, right), so shallow contents could burn because they are immediately subjected to direct heat (as compared to gradual warming).

4. HAVE CONFIDENCE

What we learned is rolled into these recipes to ensure your success. Our recipes have been tested across several slow cooker brands to ensure they work, regardless of brand. Just make sure you use the slow cooker size called for in the recipe, rotate and/or line the crockery insert as directed, and follow the shorter-than-average cook times and doneness cues to ensure that your finished recipes turn out just as well as they did in our Test Kitchen.

OPTIONS

Slow cookers come with myriad options: basic, programmable, easy-to-tote with locking lid, app-enabled to adjust cook time and temperature remotely. Sizes range from 1 to 7 quarts—smaller sizes are generally for dips. The 3½- to 5-quart range works nicely for couples, and 6-quart models hold enough to serve dinner for 4 with leftovers.

APP

ERS

LAYERS

ETIZ

Whether your gathering is planned or spur-of-the-moment, you can make these nibbles to fit your function. Fast or slow—they'll be ready when you are.

BACON DEVILED EGGS

Makes 12 servings

- 6 large eggs
- ¼ cup mayonnaise
- 3 slices bacon, crisp-cooked and crumbled
- 2 Tbsp. snipped fresh chives
- 1 Tbsp. Dijon-style mustard

  Dash cayenne pepper

FAST 8-MINUTE COOK TIME

Place a steam rack in a 6-qt. electric or stove-top pressure cooker. Add 1 cup water to pot. Place eggs in a single layer on rack. Lock lid in place. Set an electric cooker on high pressure to cook 8 minutes. For a stove-top cooker, bring up to pressure over medium-high heat; reduce heat enough to maintain steady pressure. Cook 8 minutes. Remove from heat.

For both models, release pressure quickly. Carefully open lid. Transfer eggs to a colander; run cold water over the eggs or place them in a bowl of ice water until cool enough to handle; drain. Peel off eggshells. Halve hard-cooked eggs lengthwise and remove yolks. Place yolks in a small bowl; mash with a fork. Add mayonnaise, half the bacon, the chives, mustard, and cayenne pepper. Stuff egg white halves with yolk mixture. Top with remaining bacon. If desired, sprinkle with additional snipped chives.

SLOW 2½-HOUR LOW COOK TIME

Place eggs in a single layer in a 3½- or 4-qt. slow cooker. Add enough cold water to just cover the eggs. Cover and cook on low 2½ hours. Transfer eggs to a colander; run cold water over the eggs or place them in a bowl of ice water until cool enough to handle; drain. Peel off eggshells. Halve hard-cooked eggs lengthwise and remove yolks. Place yolks in a small bowl; mash with a fork. Add mayonnaise, half the bacon, the chives, mustard, and cayenne pepper. Stuff egg white halves with yolk mixture. Top with remaining bacon. If desired, sprinkle with additional snipped chives.

GOOD EGGS

The pressure cooker turns out perfect eggs at any doneness you like. For hard-cooked eggs, set to 8 or 9 minutes; for medium-cooked eggs, set to 5 to 7 minutes; and for soft-cooked eggs, 3 to 4 minutes.

UP the flavor

Switch it up: Leave the bacon out of the yolk mixture and top with lox, sour cream, and chives.

PER SERVING *76 cal., 7 g fat (2 g sat. fat), 97 mg chol., 127 mg sodium, 0 g carb., 0 g fiber, 0 g sugars, 4 g pro.*

GARLICKY SPINACH AND FETA DIP

[VEGETARIAN]---[COMPANY]

Makes 40 servings

- 3 cloves garlic, minced
- 1 Tbsp. olive oil
- 10 oz. fresh arugula or spinach
- 8 oz. fresh spinach
- 1 8-oz. pkg. cream cheese, softened
- 1 cup plain Greek yogurt
- 1 cup mayonnaise
- ⅓ cup sliced pitted Kalamata olives
- ¼ tsp. freshly ground black pepper
- 1 cup crumbled feta cheese (4 oz.)
- ½ cup chopped green onions
- Pita chips, multigrain snack chips, and/or assorted vegetable dippers

FAST · 10-MINUTE COOK TIME

In a 6-qt. electric pressure cooker use the saute setting to cook and stir garlic in hot oil 1 minute. Gradually add arugula and spinach; cook and stir until greens will. For a stove-top cooker, cook directly in the pot over medium heat. Drain well; cool slightly. Press out any excess liquid from greens. Using kitchen scissors, snip the greens into bite-size pieces. In a large bowl combine greens, the next five ingredients (through pepper), ¾ cup of the feta, and ⅓ cup of the green onions. Transfer to a 1½-qt. round ceramic or glass baking dish. Place steam rack in pot. Add 2 cups water to pot.

From heavy foil cut three 18×3-inch foil strips; fold in half lengthwise. Crisscross strips and place dish on top of crisscross. Use strips to place dish on steam rack. Fold strips inside pot. Lock lid in place. Set electric cooker on high pressure to cook 10 minutes. For stove-top cooker, bring up to pressure over medium-high heat; reduce heat enough to maintain steady pressure. Cook 10 minutes. Remove from heat. For both models, release pressure quickly. Carefully open lid. Use foil strips to lift dish out of pot. Stir. Sprinkle with remaining feta and green onions. Serve with chips and/or vegetables.

SLOW · 1¾-HOUR LOW COOK TIME

In a 4- to 6-qt. Dutch oven cook and stir garlic in hot oil over medium heat 1 minute. Gradually add arugula and spinach; cook and stir until greens wilt. Drain well; cool slightly. Press out any excess liquid from greens. Using kitchen scissors, snip the greens into bite-size pieces. In a large bowl combine the greens, the next five ingredients (through pepper), ¾ cup of the feta, and ⅓ cup of the green onions. Transfer spinach mixture to a 1½-qt. slow cooker. Cover and cook on low 1½ hours. Stir dip; cook 15 minutes more. Sprinkle with the remaining feta and green onions. Serve immediately or keep warm on warm setting up to 2 hours. Serve with chips and/or vegetables.

TIP
Swap two 10-oz. packages frozen chopped spinach, thawed and well-drained, in place of the fresh greens.

PER 2 TBSP. DIP 83 cal., 8 g fat (3 g sat. fat), 12 mg chol., 124 mg sodium, 1 g carb., 0 g fiber, 1 g sugars, 2 g pro.

PEPPERONI PIZZA DIP

Makes 24 servings

- 1 15- to 16-oz. jar pizza sauce
- 1 14.5-oz. can diced tomatoes, drained
- 1 cup coarsely chopped yellow, orange, and/or red sweet peppers
- 1 cup coarsely chopped onion
- 1 3- to 3.5-oz. pkg. sliced pepperoni, cut up
- 1 2.25-oz. can sliced pitted ripe olives (optional)
- 4 cloves garlic, minced
- 2 cups shredded mozzarella cheese (8 oz.) or 8 oz. fresh mozzarella pearls
- ½ cup finely shredded Parmesan cheese (2 oz.)
- 2 Tbsp. basil pesto or 1 Tbsp. shredded fresh basil*
- 1 recipe Crostini (recipe p. 19)

FAST *7-MINUTE COOK TIME*

Place a steam rack in a 6-qt. electric or stove-top pressure cooker. Add 1 cup water to pot. In a 1½-qt. round ceramic or glass baking dish combine the first seven ingredients (through garlic). From heavy foil cut three 18×3-inch foil strips; fold in half lengthwise. Crisscross strips and place dish on top of crisscross. Use strips to place dish on steam rack. Fold strips inside pot. Lock lid in place. Set an electric cooker on low pressure to cook 7 minutes. For a stove-top cooker, bring up to pressure over medium heat; reduce heat to maintain steady pressure. Cook 7 minutes. Remove from heat.

For both models, let stand 15 minutes to release pressure naturally. Release any remaining pressure. Carefully open lid. Stir mozzarella cheese into dip. Let stand, covered, 10 minutes; stir. Use foil strips to lift dish out of pot. Sprinkle with Parmesan cheese. Top with pesto. Serve with crostini.

SLOW *5-HOUR LOW OR 2½-HOUR HIGH COOK TIME*

In a 3½- or 4-qt. slow cooker combine the first seven ingredients (through garlic). Cover and cook on low 5 to 6 hours or high 2½ to 3 hours. Stir in mozzarella cheese. Let stand, covered, 10 minutes; stir. Sprinkle with Parmesan cheese. Serve immediately or keep warm, covered, on warm or low up to 2 hours. Top with pesto. Serve with crostini.

*INGREDIENT KNOW-HOW
Here's how to shred or chiffonade fresh basil—it's a simple technique to create ribbons of delicate leafy greens. Simply stack the leaves, gently roll them up, then use a sharp knife to thinly slice through the roll.

PER ¼ CUP DIP *62 cal., 3 g fat (1 g sat. fat), 12 mg chol., 263 mg sodium, 4 g carb., 1 g fiber, 2 g sugars, 5 g pro.*

CARAMELIZED ONION JAM AND GOAT CHEESE CROSTINI

[VEGETARIAN]---[HEALTHY]---[COMPANY]--

Makes 24 servings

Nonstick cooking spray

4 medium onions, thinly sliced (about 4 cups)

⅓ cup red wine vinegar

¼ cup packed brown sugar

4 cloves garlic, minced

1 tsp. salt

1 recipe Crostini

4 oz. goat cheese (chèvre), softened

Snipped fresh thyme or oregano

FAST *20-MINUTE COOK TIME*

Lightly coat a 6-qt. electric or stove-top pressure cooker with cooking spray. Combine the next five ingredients (through salt) in the pot. Lock lid in place. Set an electric cooker on high pressure to cook 20 minutes. For a stove-top cooker, bring up to pressure over medium-high heat; reduce heat enough to maintain steady pressure. Cook 20 minutes. Remove from heat.

For both models, let stand 15 minutes to release pressure naturally. Release any remaining pressure. Carefully open lid. Spread crostini with cheese. Using a slotted spoon, serve caramelized onions on crostini with cheese. Sprinkle with thyme or oregano.

SLOW *12-HOUR LOW OR 6-HOUR HIGH COOK TIME*

Lightly coat a 3½- or 4-qt. slow cooker with cooking spray. In the cooker combine the next five ingredients (through salt). Cover and cook on low 12 to 14 hours or high 6 to 7 hours. Spread crostini with cheese. Using a slotted spoon, serve caramelized onions on crostini with cheese. Sprinkle with thyme or oregano.

CROSTINI

For crostini, preheat oven to 400°F. Slice 1 loaf baguette-style French bread into twenty-four ½-inch slices. Place slices on an ungreased baking sheet. Lightly coat slices with nonstick cooking spray. Bake 8 minutes or until lightly toasted.

UP the flavor

Add salty, smoky flavor to these with a crumble of crisped prosciutto on top.

PER SERVING *90 cal., 2 g fat (1 g sat. fat), 4 mg chol., 232 mg sodium, 15 g carb., 1 g fiber, 4 g sugars, 3 g pro.*

MEDJOOL DATE, PANCETTA, AND BLUE CHEESE MELT

[COMPANY]

Makes 10 servings

Nonstick cooking spray

4 oz. pancetta, finely chopped

1 shallot, thinly sliced

¾ cup chopped pitted Medjool dates

1 8-oz. pkg. cream cheese, softened

½ cup crumbled blue cheese (2 oz.)

½ cup balsamic vinegar

2 Tbsp. packed brown sugar

2 Tbsp. chopped pecans, toasted*

Crackers, melba toast rounds, and/or fresh figs

FAST *10-MINUTE COOK TIME*

Lightly coat a 1½-qt. round ceramic or glass baking dish with cooking spray. In a 6-qt. electric pressure cooker use the saute setting to cook pancetta 3 minutes. For a stove-top cooker, cook directly in the pot over medium heat. Add shallot; cook and stir 2 minutes or until pancetta is crisp. Transfer to a bowl. Add dates, cream cheese, and blue cheese; stir. Spoon cheese mixture into prepared dish. Place a steam rack in cooker. Add 1 cup water to pot. From heavy foil cut three 18×3-inch foil strips; fold in half lengthwise. Crisscross strips and place dish on top of crisscross. Use foil strips to transfer dish to steam rack. Fold strips inside pot. Lock lid in place. Set an electric cooker on high pressure to cook 10 minutes. For a stove-top cooker, bring up to pressure over medium-high heat; reduce heat enough to maintain steady pressure. Cook 10 minutes. Remove from heat. For both models, release pressure quickly. Carefully open lid. Use foil strips to lift dish out of pot. Meanwhile, in a saucepan combine vinegar and brown sugar. Bring to boiling; reduce heat. Simmer, uncovered, 5 to 7 minutes or until reduced by half. Cool. Drizzle cheese melt with balsamic reduction. Sprinkle with pecans. Serve with crackers, melba toast rounds, and/or fresh figs.

SLOW *1½-HOUR HIGH COOK TIME*

Lightly coat a 1½-qt. slow cooker with cooking spray; set aside. In a medium skillet cook and stir pancetta over medium heat 3 minutes. Add shallot; cook and stir 2 minutes more or until pancetta is crisp. Transfer to a medium bowl. Add dates, cream cheese, and blue cheese; stir. Spoon cheese mixture into prepared cooker. Cover and cook on high 1½ hours, stirring once or twice. Meanwhile, in a saucepan combine vinegar and brown sugar. Bring to boiling; reduce heat. Simmer, uncovered, 5 to 7 minutes or until reduced by half. Cool. Drizzle cheese melt with balsamic reduction. Sprinkle with pecans. Serve with crackers, melba toast rounds, and/or fresh figs.

*TIP
To toast nuts or coconut, preheat oven to 350°F. Spread nuts or coconut in a shallow baking pan. Bake 5 to 10 minutes or until lightly browned, shaking pan once or twice. Watch closely to prevent burning coconut.

PER ¼-CUP SERVING *240 cal., 16 g fat (8 g sat. fat), 36 mg chol., 281 mg sodium, 19 g carb., 1 g fiber, 16 g sugars, 5 g pro.*

LEMON-THYME STEAMED ARTICHOKES WITH BAGNA CAUDA SAUCE

Makes 4 servings

- 1 lemon
- 2 artichokes
- 1 Tbsp. minced garlic
- ½ tsp. kosher salt
- ½ tsp. freshly ground black pepper
- 1 Tbsp. olive oil
- 2 sprigs fresh thyme
- 1 recipe Bagna Cauda Sauce
- 2 tsp. snipped fresh thyme

DIRECTIONS

Remove 3 strips of zest from lemon. Cut lemon in half. Trim stems from artichokes to stand; remove loose outer leaves. Cut about 1 inch off the top of each artichoke; snip off sharp leaf tips. Rub cut edges of artichokes with a lemon half to prevent browning. Prepare as directed for desired cooker, below.

FAST 15-MINUTE COOK TIME

In a 4- to 6- qt. electric or stove-top pressure cooker place artichokes, stem ends down. Pour 1 cup water around artichokes. Squeeze lemon halves over artichokes. Sprinkle artichokes with garlic, salt, and pepper. Drizzle with oil. Add lemon strips and thyme sprigs. Lock lid in place. Set an electric cooker on high pressure to cook 15 minutes. For a stove-top cooker, bring up to pressure over medium-high heat; reduce heat enough to maintain steady pressure. Cook 15 minutes. Remove from heat.

For both models, let stand 15 minutes to release pressure naturally. Carefully open lid. Using a slotted spoon, transfer artichokes to a platter. Drizzle with 2 Tbsp. Bagna Cauda Sauce. Sprinkle with snipped thyme. Serve with remaining sauce.

SLOW 6-HOUR LOW OR 3-HOUR HIGH COOK TIME

In a 3½- or 4-qt. slow cooker place artichokes, stem ends down. Pour 1 cup water around artichokes. Squeeze lemon halves over artichokes. Sprinkle artichokes with garlic, salt, and pepper. Drizzle with oil. Add lemon strips and thyme sprigs. Cover and cook on low 6 to 7 hours or high 3 to 3½ hours or until a leaf easily pulls out of artichoke. Using a slotted spoon, transfer artichokes to a platter. Drizzle with 2 Tbsp. Bagna Cauda Sauce. Sprinkle with snipped thyme. Serve with remaining sauce.

BAGNA CAUDA SAUCE

In a small saucepan combine 1½ tsp. minced garlic; 3 Tbsp. olive oil; 2 Tbsp. butter; 2 canned anchovies, minced (2 tsp.); and ¼ tsp. crushed red pepper. Cook over low heat 5 minutes or until sauce begins to bubble. Remove from heat. Makes ⅓ cup sauce.

PER SERVING *213 cal., 20 g fat (6 g sat. fat), 17 mg chol., 317 mg sodium, 9 g carb, 4 g fiber, 1 g sugars, 3 g pro.*

GYRO NACHOS
WITH TZATZIKI SAUCE

Makes 10 servings

- 2 to 2½ lb. bone-in chicken thighs, skinned
- 1 red onion, thinly sliced
- 2 Tbsp. lemon juice
- 2 Tbsp. red wine vinegar
- 2 Tbsp. olive oil
- 6 cloves garlic, minced
- 4 tsp. dried oregano, crushed
- 1 tsp. salt
- 1 8-oz. pkg. plain pita chips*
- 1 recipe Tzatziki Sauce
- ½ cup chopped tomato

FAST *15-MINUTE COOK TIME*

In a 4- to 6-qt. electric or stove-top pressure cooker combine the first eight ingredients (through salt). Lock lid in place. Set an electric cooker on high pressure to cook 15 minutes. For a stove-top cooker, bring up to pressure over medium-high heat; reduce heat enough to maintain steady pressure. Cook 15 minutes. Remove from heat.

For both models, release pressure quickly. Carefully open lid. Remove chicken and onion from cooker using a slotted spoon. When chicken is cool enough to handle, remove bones. Shred chicken using two forks. In a bowl combine chicken and onion; add enough cooking liquid to moisten. Spread pita chips on a platter. Spoon chicken over chips. Top with Tzatziki Sauce and tomato.

SLOW *6-HOUR LOW OR 3-HOUR HIGH COOK TIME*

In a 3½- or 4-qt. slow cooker combine the first eight ingredients (through salt). Cover and cook on low 6 to 7 hours or high 3 to 3½ hours. Remove chicken and onion from cooker using a slotted spoon. When chicken is cool enough to handle, remove bones. Shred chicken using two forks. In a bowl combine chicken and onion; add enough cooking liquid to moisten. Spread pita chips on a platter. Spoon chicken over chips. Top with Tzatziki Sauce and tomato.

TZATZIKI SAUCE
In a bowl combine one 5.3- to 7-oz. carton plain Greek yogurt, 1 cup chopped cucumber, 2 tsp. snipped fresh dill weed, 2 cloves minced garlic, 1 tsp. lemon juice, and ¼ tsp. salt. Makes 1⅓ cups sauce.

*INGREDIENT KNOW-HOW
To make pita chips, lightly grease a large baking sheet. Split two 6-inch pita bread rounds in half horizontally; cut each half into wedges, strips, or rectangles. Brush with olive oil and place on baking sheet. Bake in a 350°F oven 10 to 12 minutes or until golden brown.

PER SERVING *267 cal, 11 g fat (2 g sat. fat), 82 mg chol, 523 mg sodium, 21 g carb., 3 g fiber, 3 g sugars, 21 g pro.*

BRIE AND CAMEMBERT WITH BRANDIED FRUIT

Makes 6 servings

Nonstick cooking spray

4 to 4½ oz. Brie cheese, rind removed, cut into ½- to ¾-inch cubes

2 oz. Camembert cheese, rind removed, cut into ½- to ¾-inch cubes

½ cup chopped assorted dried fruits, such as cranberries, cherries, golden raisins, and/or apricots

1 Tbsp. butter

¼ cup packed brown sugar

2 Tbsp. brandy

½ cup chopped walnuts, toasted (tip p. 20)

Crackers, crostini (recipe p. 19), and/or apple slices

FAST *3-MINUTE COOK TIME*

Place a steam rack in a 6-qt. electric or stove-top pressure cooker. Add 1 cup water to pot. Lightly coat a 1½-qt. ceramic or glass baking dish with cooking spray; add cheeses and dried fruits. In a small saucepan combine butter, sugar, and brandy. Bring to boiling; reduce heat. Simmer, uncovered, 1 minute. Pour mixture over cheese and dried fruit.

From heavy foil cut three 18×3-inch foil strips; fold in half lengthwise. Crisscross strips and place dish on top of crisscross. Use strips to place dish on steam rack. Fold strips inside pot. Lock the lid. Set an electric cooker on high pressure to cook 3 minutes. For a stove-top cooker, bring up to pressure over medium-high heat; reduce heat enough to maintain steady pressure. Cook 3 minutes. Remove from heat.

For both models, release pressure quickly. Carefully open lid. Use foil strips to lift dish out of pot. Sprinkle with walnuts. Serve warm with crackers, crostini, and/or apple slices.

SLOW *2-HOUR LOW COOK TIME*

Lightly coat a 1½-qt. slow cooker with cooking spray. Add cheeses and dried fruits. In a small saucepan combine butter, sugar, and brandy. Bring to boiling; reduce heat. Simmer, uncovered, 1 minute. Pour mixture over cheese and dried fruit. Cover and cook on low 2 to 3 hours. Sprinkle with walnuts. Serve warm with crackers, crostini, and/or apple slices.

PER ¼ CUP DIP 252 cal., 16 g fat (7 g sat. fat), 31 mg chol., 217 mg sodium, 19 g carb., 1 g fiber, 17 g sugars, 7 g pro.

ASIAN CHICKEN WINGS

Makes 12 servings

- 12 chicken wings
  (3¼ to 3½ lb.)
- ¼ tsp. salt
- ¼ tsp. black pepper
- ½ cup reduced-
  sodium chicken
  broth
- ½ cup hoisin sauce
- ¼ cup reduced-
  sodium soy sauce
- 2 Tbsp. rice vinegar
- 2 tsp. sriracha sauce

DIRECTIONS

Cut off and discard tips of chicken wings. Cut wings at joints to form 24 pieces; sprinkle with salt and pepper. Prepare as directed for desired cooker, below.

FAST *10-MINUTE COOK TIME*

In a 6-qt. electric or stove-top pressure cooker combine wing pieces and broth. Lock lid in place. Set an electric cooker on high pressure to cook 10 minutes. For a stove-top cooker, bring up to pressure over medium-high heat; reduce heat to maintain steady pressure. Cook 10 minutes. Remove from heat. For both models, release pressure quickly. Carefully open lid. Preheat broiler. Line a 15×10-inch baking pan with foil. Using tongs, transfer wings to prepared pan. Broil wings 4 to 5 inches from heat 8 minutes, turning once. Toss wings with one-fourth of desired sauce. Broil 3 to 5 minutes or until sauce is thickened and wings are lightly browned. Toss wings with another one-fourth sauce. Serve with remaining sauce.

SLOW *4-HOUR LOW OR 2-HOUR HIGH COOK TIME*

In a 3½- or 4-qt. slow cooker combine wing pieces and broth. Cover and cook on low 4 to 5 hours or high 2 to 2½ hours, stirring once halfway through. Preheat broiler. Line a 15×10-inch baking pan with foil. Using tongs, transfer wings to prepared pan; discard cooking liquid. Broil wings 4 to 5 inches from heat 8 minutes, turning once. Toss wings with one-fourth of desired sauce. Broil 3 to 5 minutes or until sauce is thickened and wings are lightly browned. Toss wings with another one-fourth sauce. Serve with remaining sauce.

HONEY-MUSTARD SAUCE
In a bowl stir together ½ cup each coarse ground mustard and honey.
PER 2 PIECES *258 cal., 17 g fat (5 g sat. fat), 61 mg chol., 228 mg sodium, 12 g carb., 0 g fiber, 11 g sugars, 15 g pro.*

APRICOT-LIME SAUCE
In a bowl stir together ¾ cup apricot preserves, 2 Tbsp. cider vinegar, 4 tsp. reduced-sodium soy sauce, and 2 tsp. grated lime zest.
PER 2 PIECES *266 cal., 17 g fat (5 g sat. fat), 60 mg chol., 167 mg sodium, 13 g carb., 0 g fiber, 9 g sugars, 15 g pro.*

BUFFALO-RANCH SAUCE
In a bowl stir together ½ cup sour cream, ⅓ cup buttermilk, ¼ cup bottled hot pepper sauce, 2 Tbsp. snipped fresh chives, 4 tsp. snipped fresh dill, and 3 cloves garlic, minced.
PER 2 PIECES *236 cal., 18 g fat (6 g sat. fat), 66 mg chol., 297 mg sodium, 1 g carb., 0 g fiber, 1 g sugars, 16 g pro.*

ASIAN SAUCE
In a bowl stir together ½ cup hoisin sauce, ¼ cup reduced-sodium soy sauce, 2 Tbsp. rice vinegar, and 2 tsp. sriracha sauce.
PER 2 PIECES *248 cal., 17 g fat (5 g sat. fat), 61 mg chol., 476 mg sodium, 6 g carb., 0 g fiber, 4 g sugars, 16 g pro.*

PICK your flavor

Top to bottom: Apricot-Lime, Honey-Mustard, Asian, Buffalo-Ranch

ASIAN CHICKEN LETTUCE WRAPS

Makes 12 servings

Nonstick cooking
spray

2 lb. uncooked
ground chicken

3 green onions

1 8-oz. can whole
water chestnuts,
drained and
chopped

1 cup shredded
carrots

1 cup frozen
edamame

3 Tbsp. reduced-
sodium soy sauce

2 Tbsp. Chinese-style
hot mustard

2 Tbsp. reduced-
sodium teriyaki
sauce

1 Tbsp. rice vinegar

¼ tsp. black pepper

1 cup reduced-
sodium chicken
broth

2 Tbsp. hoisin sauce

12 leaves butterhead
(Bibb or Boston)
lettuce or iceberg
lettuce

Asian chili-garlic
sauce (optional)

Sesame seeds
(optional)

FAST *1-MINUTE COOK TIME*

Lightly coat a 4- to 6-qt. electric or
stove-top pressure cooker with cooking
spray. For an electric cooker, use the
saute setting to cook and stir chicken
5 minutes or until no longer pink. For a
stove-top cooker, cook directly in the
pot over medium heat. Thinly slice white
portions of green onions. Bias-slice
green onion tops; set aside. Add white
portions and the next eight ingredients
(through pepper) to pot. Add broth.
Lock lid in place. Set an electric cooker
on high pressure to cook 1 minute. For a
stove-top cooker, bring up to pressure
over medium-high heat. Once up to
pressure, remove from heat.

For both models, release pressure
quickly. Carefully open lid. Strain mixture
into a serving bowl; reserving cooking
liquid. Stir hoisin sauce and green onion
tops into chicken mixture. Serve with
lettuce leaves and, if desired, Asian chili
sauce, sesame seeds, and reserved
cooking liquid for drizzling.

SLOW *4-HOUR LOW OR 2-HOUR HIGH
COOK TIME*

Lightly coat a large skillet with cooking
spray. Cook and stir chicken over
medium-high heat 5 minutes or until no
longer pink. Thinly slice white portions
of green onions. Bias-slice green onion
tops; set aside. In a 3½- or 4-qt. slow
cooker combine cooked chicken, the
white parts of green onions, and the
next eight ingredients (through pepper).
Pour broth over all. Cover and cook on
low 4 to 5 hours or high 2 to 2½ hours.

Strain mixture into a serving bowl,
reserving cooking liquid. Stir hoisin
sauce and green onion tops into chicken
mixture. Serve with lettuce leaves and,
if desired, Asian chili sauce, sesame
seeds, and reserved cooking liquid
for drizzling.

GOOD TO KNOW

*To make hot mustard, in a
bowl stir together 2 Tbsp.
mustard powder (such as
Colman's) and 2 Tbsp. cold
water. Let stand 15 minutes;
use immediately.*

PER SERVING *149 cal., 7 g fat (2 g sat. fat), 65 mg chol.,
354 mg sodium, 6 g carb., 1 g fiber, 2 g sugars, 16 g pro.*

HONEY-CHIPOTLE RIBLETS

COMPANY

Makes 12 servings

- 1 Tbsp. packed brown sugar
- 1 Tbsp. paprika
- 2 tsp. onion powder
- 1 tsp. salt
- 1 tsp. garlic powder
- 1 tsp. ground chipotle pepper or chili powder
- 3 lb. pork loin back ribs
- 1 cup ketchup
- ⅓ cup honey
- 2 Tbsp. molasses
- 1 to 2 canned chipotle peppers, minced
- 2 cloves garlic, minced

DIRECTIONS

For the rub, in a small bowl combine the first six ingredients (through ground chipotle pepper); sprinkle over ribs and rub in with your fingers. Cut ribs into single-rib portions. Prepare as directed for desired cooker, below.

FAST *22-MINUTE COOK TIME*

Place rib portions in a 6-qt. electric or stove-top pressure cooker. For sauce, in a medium bowl combine remaining ingredients. Pour ½ cup of the sauce over ribs. Lock lid in place. Set an electric cooker on high pressure to cook 22 minutes. For a stove-top cooker, bring up to pressure over medium-high heat; reduce heat enough to maintain steady pressure. Cook 22 minutes. Remove from heat.

For both models, let stand 15 minutes to release pressure naturally. Release any remaining pressure. Carefully open lid. Transfer ribs to a platter. Brush or spoon some sauce over ribs. Serve with remaining sauce.

SLOW *5-HOUR LOW OR 2½-HOUR HIGH COOK TIME*

Place rib portions in a 5- to 6-qt. slow cooker. For sauce, in a medium bowl combine remaining ingredients. Pour ½ cup of the sauce over ribs. Cover and cook on low 5 to 6 hours or on high 2½ to 3 hours. Transfer ribs to a platter. Brush or spoon some sauce over ribs. Serve with remaining sauce.

MINIMIZE THE SIZE

To make these ribs easier to handle as appetizers, ask a butcher to cut the ribs in half crosswise (across the bone) for smaller rib portions.

PER SERVING *167 cal., 6 g fat (2 g sat. fat), 37 mg chol., 445 mg sodium, 18 g carb., 0 g fiber, 16 g sugars, 12 g pro.*

SWEET-SOUR MEATBALLS

Makes 12 servings

- ¾ cup apple jelly
- 1½ tsp. Worcestershire sauce
- 1 tsp. spicy brown mustard
- Dash bottled hot pepper sauce
- 1 egg, lightly beaten
- ¼ cup fine dry bread crumbs
- ¼ cup finely chopped onion
- 2 Tbsp. milk
- ¼ tsp. salt
- ¼ tsp. black pepper
- 8 oz. bulk pork sausage
- 8 oz. ground beef
- Nonstick cooking spray or 2 Tbsp. vegetable oil
- Crushed red pepper (optional)

DIRECTIONS

For the sauce, in a small bowl stir together the first four ingredients (through hot pepper sauce). Set aside. In a large bowl combine the next six ingredients (through pepper). Add sausage and ground beef; mix well. Shape mixture into thirty-six 1-inch meatballs. Prepare as directed for desired cooker, below.

FAST   *6-MINUTE COOK TIME*

Heat a 4- to 6-qt. electric slow cooker* using the saute setting. For a stove-top cooker,* heat over medium heat. Coat bottom of the pot with cooking spray or 1 Tbsp. of the oil. Cook meatballs in cooker, half at a time, until browned, turning to brown evenly. Drain off fat.

Return meatballs to cooker. Pour sauce over meatballs; stir to coat. Lock lid in place. Set an electric pressure cooker on high pressure to cook 2 minutes. For a stove-top cooker, bring up to pressure over medium-high heat; reduce heat enough to maintain steady pressure. Cook 2 minutes. Remove from heat. For both models, release pressure quickly. Carefully open lid. If desired, sprinkle with crushed red pepper.

SLOW   *3-HOUR LOW OR 1½-HOUR HIGH COOK TIME*

Coat a large nonstick skillet* with cooking spray; heat over medium heat. Cook meatballs, half at a time, until browned, turning to brown evenly. Drain off fat.

Place meatballs in a 1½- or 2-qt. slow cooker. Pour sauce over meatballs. Cover and cook on low 3 to 4 hours or on high 1½ to 2 hours. If no heat setting is available, cook 3 to 4 hours. Serve immediately or keep warm, covered, on warm- or low-heat setting up to 2 hours. If desired, sprinkle with crushed red pepper.

*OVEN BROWNING

Preheat oven to 375°F. Lightly coat a 15×10-inch baking pan with cooking spray. Place meatballs in prepared pan. Bake 12 to 15 minutes or until meatballs are browned. Drain off fat. Continue as directed.

PER 3 MEATBALLS 178 cal., 9 g fat (3 g sat. fat), 42 mg chol., 246 mg sodium, 17 g carb., 0 g fiber, 11 g sugars, 7 g pro.

BREA
ST

AKFA

On mornings when you have time for more than a bowl of cereal or a smoothie, a pressure cooker or slow cooker can help whip up a special breakfast or brunch for family or friends.

BLUEBERRY FRENCH TOAST CASSEROLE WITH LEMON MASCARPONE CREAM

[VEGETARIAN] [COMPANY]

Makes 8 servings

- 1 12-oz. oblong loaf crusty Italian bread, cut into 1-inch slices and dried (tip p. 274)
- 2 cups frozen blueberries
- 1½ cups whole milk or reduced-fat milk
- 4 eggs
- ¼ cup heavy cream
- ¼ cup honey
- 2 tsp. vanilla
- 1 tsp. ground cinnamon
- 1 recipe Lemon Mascarpone Cream

DIRECTIONS

Grease a 1½-qt. round ceramic or glass dish. Arrange one-third of the bread slices in an even layer in prepared dish, cutting to fit. Top with half the blueberries. Repeat layers using half the remaining bread slices and all remaining blueberries. Top with remaining bread slices. In a large bowl whisk together the next six ingredients (through cinnamon). Pour over bread in dish. (Dish will be very full.) Use the back of a large spoon to press down bread to moisten top completely. Cover dish with foil. Let stand in refrigerator 30 minutes. Prepare as directed for desired cooker, below.

FAST *25-MINUTE COOK TIME*

Place a steam rack in a 6-qt. electric or stove-top pressure cooker. Add 1½ cups water to pot. From heavy foil cut three 18×3-inch foil strips; fold in half lengthwise. Crisscross strips and place dish on top of crisscross. Use strips to place dish on steam rack. Fold strips inside pot. Lock lid in place. Set an electric cooker on high pressure to cook 25 minutes. For a stove-top cooker, bring up to pressure over medium-high heat; reduce heat enough to maintain steady pressure. Cook 25 minutes. Remove from heat. For both models, release pressure quickly. Carefully open lid. Use foil strips to lift dish out of pot. Let stand, loosely covered, 30 minutes. Serve with Lemon Mascarpone Cream.

SLOW *5-HOUR LOW COOK TIME*

Place dish in a 6-qt. slow cooker. Cover and cook on low 5 to 6 hours or until a knife inserted in the center comes out clean (160°F). Remove crockery liner from cooker, if possible, or turn off cooker. Let stand, loosely covered, 30 minutes. Serve with Lemon Mascarpone Cream.

LEMON MASCARPONE CREAM
Remove 2 tsp. grated zest and 1 Tbsp. juice from a lemon. In a chilled medium bowl beat ⅔ cup heavy cream on medium until soft peaks form. In another medium bowl beat ¾ cup mascarpone cheese or cream cheese, ¼ cup honey, the lemon zest and juice, and ⅛ tsp. nutmeg on medium until well combined. Fold about one-third of the whipped cream into mascarpone mixture. Fold in remaining whipped cream.

PER SERVING *451 cal., 25 g fat (13 g sat. fat), 159 mg chol., 305 mg sodium, 47 g carb., 3 g fiber, 25 g sugars, 10 g pro.*

BACON, CORN, AND CHEESE FRITTATA

COMPANY

Makes 4 servings

Nonstick cooking spray

6 eggs, lightly beaten

¾ cup fresh or frozen whole kernel corn, thawed

½ cup thinly sliced green onions

6 slices bacon, crisp-cooked and crumbled

¼ cup finely chopped roasted red sweet peppers

¼ cup half-and-half

½ tsp. freshly ground black pepper

¼ tsp. salt

¾ cup shredded Monterey Jack cheese with jalapeño peppers (3 oz.)

¼ cup chopped fresh chives or Italian parsley

DIRECTIONS

Lightly coat a 1½-qt. soufflé dish or round casserole with cooking spray. In a medium bowl combine the next eight ingredients (through salt). Stir in ½ cup of the cheese. Transfer egg mixture to prepared dish. Top with remaining ¼ cup cheese. Prepare as directed for desired cooker, below.

FAST *18-MINUTE COOK TIME*

Place a steam rack in a 5- to 6-qt. electric or stove-top pressure cooker. Add 1 cup water to pot. Place filled dish on rack. Lock lid in place. Set an electric cooker on high pressure to cook 18 minutes. For a stove-top cooker, bring up to pressure over medium-high heat; reduce heat enough to maintain steady pressure. Cook 18 minutes. Remove from heat.

For both models, let stand 15 minutes to naturally release pressure. Release any remaining pressure. Carefully open lid. Let stand 10 minutes. Sprinkle with chives.

SLOW *2-HOUR HIGH COOK TIME*

Place dish in a 5- to 6-qt. slow cooker. Cover and cook on high 2 to 2½ hours or until frittata is set. (Frittata will puff during cooking and settle when cooling.) Let stand 10 minutes. Sprinkle with chives.

UP the flavor

For smoky flavor, swap the Monterey Jack for smoked cheddar or Gouda.

PER SERVING *303 cal., 19 g fat (9 g sat. fat), 315 mg chol., 639 mg sodium, 10 g carb., 1 g fiber, 3 g sugars, 20 g pro.*

BUTTERNUT SQUASH
SHAKSHUKA

Makes 6 servings

- ¾ cup chopped red sweet pepper
- 1 small onion, halved and thinly sliced
- 1 medium jalapeño pepper,* seeded and finely chopped
- 2 cloves garlic, minced
- 1 tsp. dried oregano, crushed
- 1 tsp. ground cumin
- ½ tsp. salt
- ½ tsp. black pepper
- 1 2-lb. butternut squash, peeled, seeded, and chopped (about 6 cups)
- 1 15-oz. can or ½ of a 28-oz. can crushed tomatoes
- 1 8-oz. can tomato sauce
- 6 eggs
- ¾ cup crumbled feta cheese (3 oz.)
- 2 Tbsp. snipped fresh Italian parsley
- Pita bread rounds, warmed

FAST *6-MINUTE COOK TIME*

In a 6-qt. electric or stovetop pressure cooker combine first eight ingredients (through black pepper). Stir in squash, crushed tomatoes, and tomato sauce. Lock lid in place. Set an electric cooker on high pressure to cook 5 minutes. For a stove-top cooker, bring up to pressure over medium-high heat; reduce heat enough to maintain steady pressure. Cook 5 minutes. Remove from heat.

For both models, release pressure quickly. Carefully open lid. Break one egg into a custard cup. Make an indentation in squash mixture; slide egg into indentation. Repeat with remaining eggs. Lock lid in place. Set an electric cooker on high pressure to cook 1 minute. For a stove-top cooker, bring up to pressure over medium-high heat. As soon as pressure is reached, turn off cooker and remove from heat. For both models, release pressure quickly. Carefully open lid. If desired, cover and let stand until eggs are desired doneness. Top servings with cheese and parsley. Serve with pita bread.

SLOW *11-HOUR LOW OR 5½-HOUR HIGH COOK TIME + 25 MINUTES HIGH*

In a 3½- or 4-qt. slow cooker combine first eight ingredients (through black pepper). Stir in squash, crushed tomatoes, and tomato sauce. Cover and cook on low 11 to 12 hours or high 5½ to 6 hours. If using low, turn to high. Break an egg into a custard cup. Make an indentation in squash mixture; slide egg into indentation. Repeat with remaining eggs. Cover and cook 25 to 35 minutes more or until eggs are desired doneness. Top servings with cheese and parsley. Serve with pita bread.

***CHILE PEPPER TIP**
Chile peppers contain oils that can irritate skin and eyes. Wear plastic or rubber gloves when working with them.

PER SERVING *315 cal., 10 g fat (5 g sat. fat), 203 mg chol., 917 mg sodium, 45 g carb., 6 g fiber, 10 g sugars, 15 g pro.*

MEXICAN POTATO
BREAKFAST CASSEROLE

Makes 8 servings

Nonstick cooking spray

3 cups frozen shredded hash brown potatoes

1 cup reduced-sodium black beans, rinsed and drained

½ cup chopped red sweet pepper

2 green onions, thinly sliced

1½ cups shredded Mexican-style cheese blend (6 oz.)

5 eggs

¾ cup sour cream

¼ cup half-and-half

1½ tsp. chili powder

¼ tsp. salt

¼ tsp. black pepper

½ cup fresh cilantro leaves

Fresh pico de gallo

DIRECTIONS

Lightly coat a 1½-qt. round ceramic or glass baking dish with cooking spray; set aside. In a large bowl combine the next four ingredients (through green onions). Stir in 1 cup of the cheese. In a medium bowl whisk together eggs, ¼ cup of the sour cream, the half-and-half, chili powder, salt, and black pepper. Pour egg mixture over potato mixture in bowl; stir. Transfer mixture to prepared dish. Top with remaining ½ cup cheese. Prepare as directed for desired cooker, below.

FAST *22-MINUTE COOK TIME*

Place a steam rack in a 6-qt. electric or stove-top pressure cooker. Add 1 cup water to pot. From heavy foil cut three 18×3-inch foil strips; fold in half lengthwise. Crisscross strips and place dish on top of crisscross. Use strips to place dish on steam rack. Fold strips inside pot. Lock lid in place. Set an electric cooker on high pressure to cook 22 minutes. For a stove-top cooker, bring up to pressure over medium-high heat; reduce heat enough to maintain steady pressure. Cook 22 minutes. Remove from heat.

For both models, let stand 15 minutes to naturally release pressure. Release any remaining pressure. Carefully open lid. Use foil strips to lift dish out of pot. Let stand 10 minutes. Sprinkle with cilantro and serve with remaining sour cream and the pico de gallo.

SLOW *2½-HOUR HIGH COOK TIME*

Add 1 cup water to a 6-qt. slow cooker. Place filled dish in cooker. Cover and cook on high 2½ to 3 hours or until a knife inserted near center comes out clean. Carefully remove dish from cooker. Let stand 10 minutes. Sprinkle with cilantro and serve with remaining sour cream and the pico de gallo.

PER SERVING 227 cal., 14 g fat (7 g sat. fat), 149 mg chol., 393 mg sodium, 15 g carb., 3 g fiber, 3 g sugars, 12 g pro.

SCRAMBLED BREAKFAST HASH

Makes 6 servings

- 6 slices bacon, chopped
- 1 8-oz. pkg. fresh button mushrooms, sliced
- ½ cup chopped onion

  Nonstick cooking spray (slow cooker only)
- 1½ lb. Yukon gold potatoes, cut into ½-inch chunks
- ½ cup chopped red sweet pepper
- ½ tsp. salt
- ½ tsp. dried thyme, crushed
- ¼ tsp. crushed red pepper
- 6 eggs
- 3 Tbsp. milk
- ¾ cup shredded aged Gouda, Gruyère, or cheddar cheese (3 oz.)
- 1 Tbsp. snipped fresh chives

FAST *5-MINUTE COOK TIME*

In a 6-qt. electric pressure cooker use the saute setting to cook bacon over medium heat 7 to 8 minutes or until crisp. For a stove-top cooker, cook directly in the pot. Transfer bacon to paper towels to drain; cover and refrigerate until needed. Drain and discard all but 1 Tbsp. drippings from pot. Add mushrooms and onion to pot. Cook 5 to 7 minutes or until onion is tender and liquid is almost evaporated. Add potatoes, sweet pepper, salt, thyme, and crushed red pepper. Lock lid in place. Set an electric cooker on high pressure to cook 5 minutes. For a stove-top cooker, bring up to pressure over medium-high heat; reduce heat enough to maintain steady pressure. Cook 5 minutes. Remove from heat.

For both models, let stand 15 minutes to release pressure naturally. Release any remaining pressure. Carefully open lid. Drain and discard liquid. Return potato mixture to pot. In a medium bowl whisk together eggs and milk; pour over potato mixture. For an electric cooker, cook on saute setting 3 to 5 minutes or until eggs are nearly set, stirring once or twice. For a stove-top cooker, cook over medium heat. Remove from heat. Top with cheese. Cover; let stand 5 minutes. Sprinkle with bacon and chives.

SLOW *5-HOUR LOW OR 2½-HOUR HIGH COOK TIME + 45 MINUTES HIGH*

In a large skillet cook bacon over medium heat until crisp. Transfer bacon to paper towels to drain; cover and refrigerate until needed. Drain and discard all but 1 Tbsp. drippings from skillet. Add mushrooms and onion to skillet. Cook over medium heat 5 to 7 minutes or until onion is tender and liquid is almost evaporated. Lightly coat a 3½- or 4-qt. slow cooker with cooking spray. Transfer mushroom mixture to prepared cooker. Add potatoes, sweet pepper, salt, thyme, and crushed red pepper.

Cover and cook on low 5 to 6 hours or high 2½ to 3 hours or until potatoes are tender. In a medium bowl whisk together eggs and milk; pour over potato mixture in cooker. Sprinkle with cheese. If using low, turn to high. Cover and cook 45 to 50 minutes more or just until eggs are set (160°F) and cheese is melted. Remove crockery liner. Cover; let stand 5 minutes. Sprinkle with bacon and chives.

UP the flavor
Top servings with microgreens lightly dressed with vinaigrette.

PER SERVING *279 cal., 14 g fat (6 g sat. fat), 213 mg chol., 542 mg sodium, 22 g carb., 4 g fiber, 4 g sugars, 16 g pro.*

SOUTHERN TOT CASSEROLE

Makes 8 servings

- 8 oz. cooked pork breakfast sausage links or uncooked bulk pork sausage
- 1 Tbsp. vegetable oil
- 6 eggs, lightly beaten
- 1 cup heavy cream
- 1 4-oz. jar diced pimiento, drained
- ¼ tsp. ground mustard
- ¼ cup finely chopped onion
- 2 cups shredded cheddar cheese (8 oz.)
- 1 28-oz. bag frozen miniature fried potato nuggets
- ¼ cup sliced green onions

  Bottled hot pepper sauce

FAST *30-MINUTE COOK TIME*

In a 6-qt. electric pressure cooker use the saute setting to cook sausage links in hot oil 5 minutes or until browned, turning once. For a stove-top cooker, cook directly in the pot. Drain off fat. Cut links into ¼-inch slices; return to pot. Add the next five ingredients (through finely chopped onion) and half the cheese to the pot. Stir well. Add frozen potato nuggets; stir. Lock lid in place. Set an electric cooker on high pressure to cook 30 minutes. For a stove-top cooker, bring up to pressure over medium-high heat; reduce heat enough to maintain steady pressure. Cook 30 minutes. Remove from heat.

For both models, let stand 15 minutes to release pressure naturally. Release any remaining pressure. Carefully open lid. Sprinkle with remaining cheese and the green onions. Pass hot sauce.

SLOW *2¾-HOUR HIGH COOK TIME*

In a medium skillet cook sausage links in hot oil over medium-high heat 5 minutes or until browned, turning once. Cut links into ¼-inch slices. In a large bowl whisk together the next five ingredients (through finely chopped onion) and half the cheese. Add frozen potato nuggets and sausage. Pour into a 6-qt. slow cooker. Cover and cook on high 2¾ to 3 hours or until potatoes are cooked and eggs are set, turning cookery liner once halfway through cooking. Sprinkle with remaining cheese and the green onions. Pass hot sauce.

PER SERVING 593 cal., 46 g fat (18 g sat. fat), 222 mg chol., 1,027 mg sodium, 30 g carb., 3 g fiber, 3 g sugars, 19 g pro.

CHILAQUILES

Makes 6 servings

- 1½ lb. lean ground beef and/or lean ground pork
- ½ cup chopped onion
- 2 cloves garlic, minced
- 1 15.5-oz. can chili beans in chili gravy, undrained
- 1 10-oz. can enchilada sauce
- ½ cup 50%-less sodium beef broth
- 1 2.25-oz. can sliced pitted ripe olives, drained
- 1 4.5- to 4.8-oz. pkg. tostada shells, broken, or 4 cups tortilla chips
- 2 cups shredded Monterey Jack cheese (8 oz.)

  Halved cherry tomatoes, sliced fresh chile peppers (tip p. 42), salsa, sour cream, and/or snipped fresh cilantro (optional)

FAST *1-MINUTE COOK TIME*

In a 6-qt. electric pressure cooker use the saute setting to cook beef, onion, and garlic over medium-high heat 5 minutes or until meat is browned. Drain off fat. For a stove-top cooker, cook directly in the pot over medium-high heat. Add the next four ingredients (through olives). Stir in tostada shells. Lock lid in place. Set an electric cooker on high pressure to cook 1 minute. For a stove-top cooker, bring up to pressure over medium-high heat. Remove from heat once pressure is reached.

For both models, release pressure quickly. Carefully open lid. Stir in cheese; let stand 5 minutes. If desired, top servings with tomatoes, chile peppers, salsa, sour cream, and/or cilantro, and serve with additional broken tostada shells or tortilla chips.

SLOW *4-HOUR LOW COOK TIME*

In a large skillet cook beef, onion, and garlic over medium-high heat until meat is browned. Drain off fat. Line a 3½- or 4-qt. slow cooker with a disposable slow cooker liner. In prepared cooker combine the next four ingredients (through olives). Stir in meat mixture, tostada shells, and cheese.

Cover and cook on low 4 hours, giving crockery liner a half-turn halfway through, if possible. Turn off cooker. If possible, remove crockery liner from cooker. Let stand, uncovered, 30 minutes. If desired, top servings with tomatoes, chile peppers, salsa, sour cream, and/or cilantro, and serve with additional broken tostada shells or tortilla chips.

PER SERVING *555 cal., 33 g fat (14 g sat. fat), 108 mg chol., 1,074 mg sodium, 32 g carb., 6 g fiber, 2 g sugars, 37 g pro.*

SAVORY BREAKFAST CONGEE

Makes 8 servings

Nonstick cooking spray

1 lb. skinless, boneless chicken thighs

8 cups reduced-sodium chicken broth

1 cup jasmine rice, rinsed and drained

1 shallot, minced

2 cloves garlic, minced

2 tsp. grated fresh ginger

8 poached eggs*

Sliced avocado, fresh cilantro, sliced green onions, and/or bottled hot pepper sauce

FAST *20-MINUTE COOK TIME*

In a 6-qt. electric or stove-top pressure cooker combine chicken and the next five ingredients (through ginger). Lock lid in place. Set an electric cooker on high pressure to cook 20 minutes. For a stove-top cooker, bring up to pressure over medium-high heat; reduce heat enough to maintain steady pressure. Cook 20 minutes. Remove from heat.

For both models, let stand 15 minutes to release pressure naturally. Release any remaining pressure. Carefully open lid. Transfer chicken to a cutting board; shred with two forks into large pieces. Stir shredded chicken into rice mixture. Serve hot in bowls and top with poached egg, avocado, cilantro, green onions, and/or hot sauce.

SLOW *6-HOUR LOW OR 3-HOUR HIGH COOK TIME*

Lightly coat a 3½- or 4-qt. slow cooker with cooking spray. Add the next six ingredients (through ginger). Cover and cook on low 6 to 7 hours or high 3 to 3½ hours. Transfer chicken to a cutting board; shred with two forks into large pieces. Stir shredded chicken into rice mixture. Serve hot in bowls and top with poached egg, avocado, cilantro, green onions, and/or hot sauce.

*POACHED EGGS
In an extra-large skillet combine 8 cups water and 2 Tbsp. vinegar. Bring to boiling; reduce heat to simmering (bubbles should begin to break surface of water). Break an egg into a cup and slip egg into simmering water. Repeat with seven more eggs, allowing each egg equal amount of space in skillet. Simmer, uncovered, 3 to 5 minutes or until the whites are completely set and yolks begin to thicken but are not hard. Using a slotted spoon, remove eggs. Season to taste with salt and black pepper.

PER SERVING 271 cal., 10 g fat (3 g sat. fat), 238 mg chol., 777 mg sodium, 22 g carb., 1 g fiber, 1 g sugars, 23 g pro.

BACON AND EGGS
BREAKFAST BOWLS

Makes 4 servings

- 1½ cups steel-cut oats
- 4½ cups water
- ½ tsp. salt
- 1 Tbsp. butter
- 1 recipe Over-Easy Fried Eggs
- ½ cup shredded sharp cheddar cheese (2 oz.)
- 4 slices bacon, crisp-cooked and crumbled
- 1 medium avocado, halved, seeded, peeled, and sliced
- 2 Tbsp. thinly sliced green onions
  Bottled hot pepper sauce (optional)

FAST *10-MINUTE COOK TIME*

In a 4- to 6-qt. electric or stove-top pressure cooker combine oats, the water, and salt. Lock lid in place. Set an electric cooker on high pressure to cook 10 minutes. For a stove-top cooker, bring up to pressure over medium-high heat; reduce heat enough to maintain steady pressure. Cook 10 minutes. Remove from heat.

For both models, let stand 15 minutes to release pressure naturally. Carefully open lid. Stir in butter. Spoon oatmeal into bowls. Top with fried eggs, cheese, bacon, avocado, and green onions. If desired, serve with hot sauce.

SLOW *5½-HOUR LOW OR 2¾-HOUR HIGH COOK TIME*

In a 3½- or 4-qt. slow cooker combine oats, the water, and salt. Cover and cook on low 5½ to 6½ hours or high 2¾ to 3¼ hours. Stir in butter. Spoon oatmeal into bowls. Top with fried eggs, cheese, bacon, avocado, and green onions. If desired, serve with hot sauce.

OVER-EASY FRIED EGGS
In a large nonstick skillet melt 2 tsp. butter over medium heat. Break 4 eggs into skillet. If desired, sprinkle with salt and pepper. Reduce heat to low; cook eggs 3 to 4 minutes or until whites are completely set and yolks start to thicken. Turn eggs and cook 30 to 60 seconds more.

PER 1 CUP PLUS TOPPINGS *520 cal., 27 g fat (10 g sat. fat), 221 mg chol., 636 mg sodium, 48 g carb., 10 g fiber, 0 g sugars, 23 g pro.*

PEACHES AND CREAM
BREAKFAST QUINOA

VEGETARIAN

Makes 8 servings

- 4 cups water
- 2 cups uncooked white quinoa, rinsed and drained
- 3 cups chopped peeled fresh peaches or frozen sliced peaches, thawed
- ¼ cup peach preserves
- 2 tsp. vanilla
- ¾ tsp. salt
- ½ cup heavy cream
- ½ cup chopped toasted pecans (tip p. 20) (optional)
- Honey or brown sugar (optional)
- Heavy cream or milk (optional)

FAST *1-MINUTE COOK TIME*

In a 4-qt. electric or stove-top pressure cooker combine the first six ingredients (through salt). Lock lid in place. Set an electric cooker on high pressure to cook 1 minute. For a stove-top cooker, bring up to pressure over medium-high heat; reduce heat enough to maintain steady pressure. Cook 1 minute. Remove from heat.

For both models, let stand 15 minutes to release pressure naturally. Release any remaining pressure. Carefully open lid. Stir in cream. If desired, top servings with pecans and drizzle with honey and/or additional cream.

SLOW *2½-HOUR LOW OR 1½-HOUR HIGH COOK TIME*

In a 3½- or 4-qt. slow cooker combine the first six ingredients (through salt). Cover and cook on low 2½ to 3 hours or high 1½ hours. Stir in cream. If desired, top servings with pecans and drizzle with honey and/or additional cream.

UP the flavor

Top servings with slivered fresh basil, a natural complement to peaches.

PER 1 CUP *261 cal., 8 g fat (4 g sat. fat), 17 mg chol., 231 mg sodium, 40 g carb., 4 g fiber, 10 g sugars, 7 g pro.*

MULTIGRAIN HONEY-ALMOND
BREAKFAST CEREAL

Makes 8 servings

½ cup steel-cut oats

½ cup long grain brown rice

½ cup regular barley

½ cup corn grits

¼ cup millet

¼ cup honey

1 tsp. ground cinnamon

1 tsp. vanilla

½ tsp. salt

Milk

¼ cup sliced almonds, toasted (tip p. 20)

Blueberries, raspberries, sliced strawberries, and/or sliced peaches

FAST *14-MINUTE COOK TIME*

In a 6-qt. electric or stove-top pressure cooker stir together 6 cups water and the next nine ingredients (through salt). Lock lid in place. Set an electric cooker on high pressure to cook 14 minutes. For a stove-top cooker, bring up to pressure over medium-high heat; reduce heat enough to maintain steady pressure. Cook 14 minutes. Remove from heat.

For both models, quickly release pressure. Carefully open lid. Serve with milk, almonds, and fruit.

SLOW *5-HOUR LOW OR 2½-HOUR HIGH COOK TIME*

In a 3½- or 4-qt. slow cooker stir together 8 cups water and the next nine ingredients (through salt). Cover and cook on low 5 to 6 hours or high 2½ to 3 hours or until grains are tender. Serve with milk, almonds, and fruit.

KNOW YOUR OATS

Steel-cut oats are made from whole groats that are cut in tiny pieces rather than rolled. They take longer to cook than rolled oats—ideal for speeding up in a pressure cooker— and they have a chewy, toothsome texture.

PER 1¼ CUPS *254 cal, 4 g fat (1 g sat. fat), 1 mg chol, 163 mg sodium, 50 g carb, 6 g fiber, 12 g sugars, 7 g pro.*

CHAI-MAPLE CIDER

Makes 6 servings

- 4 long strips orange zest
- 2 or 3 cinnamon sticks
- 8 whole cloves
- 3 green cardamom pods
- 25 whole black peppercorns
- 5 cups apple cider
- 1 cup water
- ½ cup pure maple syrup
- 8 black tea bags
- Cinnamon sticks (optional)

DIRECTIONS

For spice bag, place the first five ingredients (through peppercorns) in the center of a double-thick, 6- to 8-inch square of 100%-cotton cheesecloth. Bring up corners; tie closed with clean kitchen string. Prepare as directed for desired cooker, below.

FAST *5-MINUTE COOK TIME*

In a 6-qt. electric or stove-top pressure cooker combine spice bag, apple cider, the water, and syrup. Lock lid in place. Set an electric cooker on high pressure to cook 5 minutes. For a stove-top cooker, bring up to pressure over medium-high heat; reduce heat enough to maintain steady pressure. Cook 5 minutes. Remove from heat.

For both models, let stand 5 minutes to release pressure naturally. Release any remaining pressure. Carefully open lid. Add tea bags, draping strings over side of cooker. Cover; let stand 10 minutes. Remove tea bags; gently press tea bags against side of cooker to release liquid. Discard tea bags and spice bag. Ladle cider into mugs and, if desired, serve with an additional cinnamon stick.

SLOW *5-HOUR LOW COOK TIME*

In a 3- to 4-qt. slow cooker combine spice bag, apple cider, the water, and syrup. Cover and cook on low 5 to 6 hours. Add tea bags, draping strings over side of cooker. Cover; let stand 10 minutes. Remove tea bags; gently press tea bags against side of cooker to release liquid. Discard tea bags and spice bag. Ladle cider into mugs and, if desired, serve with an additional cinnamon stick.

PER ¾ CUP 171 cal., 0 g fat, 0 mg chol., 32 mg sodium, 42 g carb., 0 g fiber, 38 g sugars, 0 g pro.

RIBS&
OAST.

&ROASTS

Start with hefty hunks of meat and turn them into juicy, butter-knife-tender bites of lusciousness—in a flash or on a low, slow simmer.

ASIAN BEEF SHANKS AND VEGETABLES

[WEEKNIGHT] ---[COMPANY]--

Makes 4 servings

- 3 lb. beef shank cross cuts, cut 1 inch thick; or 4 to 6 bone-in beef short ribs
- ½ tsp. salt
- ¼ tsp. black pepper
- 1 Tbsp. olive oil
- 8 oz. button mushrooms, quartered
- 2 medium carrots, cut into 2-inch pieces
- 1 large onion, cut into ½-inch wedges
- 2 cloves garlic, sliced
- 1 cup 50%-less-sodium beef broth
- 2 Tbsp. quick-cooking tapioca, crushed (slow cooker only)
- 2 Tbsp. packed brown sugar
- 2 Tbsp. reduced-sodium soy sauce
- 1 tsp. ground ginger
- 1 tsp. Chinese five-spice powder
- 1 to 2 dried Thai chile peppers (optional)
- 1 Tbsp. cornstarch (pressure cooker only)
- 8 oz. baby bok choy, halved or quartered lengthwise
- 2 cups hot cooked rice

FAST 30-MINUTE COOK TIME

Sprinkle meat with ¼ tsp. salt and the black pepper. In a 6-qt. electric pressure cooker use the saute setting to cook meat in oil until browned. For a stove-top cooker, cook meat in hot oil directly in the pot over medium-high heat. Drain off fat. Add mushrooms, carrots, onion, and garlic. Stir in broth, brown sugar, soy sauce, ginger, five-spice powder, chiles, and remaining and remaining ¼ tsp. salt. Lock lid in place. Set electric cooker on high pressure to cook 30 minutes. For a stove-top cooker, bring up to pressure over medium-high heat; reduce heat enough to maintain steady pressure. Cook 30 minutes. Remove from heat.

For both models, let stand 15 minutes to release pressure naturally. Release any remaining pressure. Carefully open lid. Using a slotted spoon, remove meat and vegetables; discard bones. For sauce, combine 1 Tbsp. each cornstarch and cold water; stir into cooking liquid. For electric cooker, heat to simmering on saute setting; for stove-top cooker, bring to simmering over medium heat. Cook and stir until thickened and bubbly. Add bok choy. Simmer, covered, 5 minutes. Combine meat and vegetables with sauce and serve over rice.

SLOW 8-HOUR LOW OR 4-HOUR HIGH COOK TIME + 30 MINUTES HIGH

Sprinkle meat with ¼ tsp. salt and the black pepper. In an extra-large skillet heat oil over medium-high heat. Add meat, half at a time, and cook until browned. Drain off fat. Transfer meat to a 5- to 6-qt. slow cooker. Add mushrooms, carrots, onion, and garlic. In a small bowl combine the next seven ingredients (through chiles) and remaining ¼ tsp. salt. Pour over meat and vegetables in cooker. Cover and cook on low 8 to 10 hours for shanks (10 to 12 hours for ribs) or high 4 to 5 hours for shanks (5 to 6 hours for ribs). If using low, turn to high. Stir in bok choy. Cover and cook 30 minutes more. Remove and discard bones. Serve meat and vegetables over rice.

SHANKS VS. RIBS

Beef shank cross cuts are cut from the leg while short ribs are—as the name implies— cut from ribs. Short ribs are meatier than shanks; both require braising for tender results.

PER SERVING *496 cal., 10 g fat (2 g sat. fat), 78 mg chol., 861 mg sodium, 48 g carb., 3 g fiber, 14 g sugars, 51 g pro.*

KOREAN-STYLE SHORT RIBS

Makes 6 servings

- 2 Tbsp. sesame oil
- 6 beef short ribs (3½ to 4 lb. total)
- ⅓ cup apple juice
- ¼ cup soy sauce
- 1 cooking apple, cored and shredded
- 2 Tbsp. packed brown sugar
- 2 Tbsp. minced garlic
- 2 Tbsp. sesame seeds, toasted

  Sliced green onions

  Hot cooked rice

  Kimchi (optional)

FAST *30-MINUTE COOK TIME*

In a 6-qt. electric pressure cooker use the saute setting to cook ribs, half at a time, in hot oil until browned on all sides. For a stove-top cooker, cook directly in pot over medium-high heat. In a bowl combine the next five ingredients (through garlic). Pour over ribs. Lock lid in place. Set an electric cooker on high pressure to cook 30 minutes. For a stove-top cooker, bring up to pressure over medium-high heat; reduce heat enough to maintain steady pressure. Cook 30 minutes. Remove from heat.

For both models, let stand 15 minutes to release pressure naturally. Release any remaining pressure. Carefully open lid. Remove ribs from cooker; discard bones. Strain cooking liquid. Skim fat from reserved liquid. Serve over ribs. Sprinkle with sesame seeds and green onions. Serve liquid with rice and, if desired, kimchi.

SLOW *7-HOUR LOW OR 3½-HOUR HIGH COOK TIME*

In an extra-large skillet cook meat in hot oil over medium-high heat until browned, turning occasionally. Transfer to a 3½- or 4-qt. slow cooker. In a bowl combine the next five ingredients (through garlic). Pour over ribs. Cover and cook on low 7 to 8 hours or high 3½ to 4 hours. Remove ribs from cooker. Discard bones. Strain cooking liquid. Skim fat off reserved liquid. Serve over ribs. Sprinkle with sesame seeds and green onions. Serve liquid with rice and, if desired, kimchi.

TOASTING SESAME SEEDS

Sesame seeds take on a wonderfully nutty flavor when toasted. Toast them in a dry skillet over medium heat 3 to 5 minutes or until lightly browned, stirring occasionally.

PER SERVING *844 cal., 64 g fat (25 g sat. fat), 133 mg chol., 759 mg sodium, 35 g carb., 2 g fiber, 9 g sugars, 32 g pro.*

SHORT RIB GOULASH

[WEEKNIGHT] --- [COMPANY]

Makes 8 servings

- 8 bone-in beef short ribs (3¾ to 4½ lb. total), trimmed
- 1 Tbsp. paprika
- 2 tsp. kosher salt
- ¼ tsp. freshly ground black pepper
- 2 Tbsp. olive oil
- 1 2-lb. butternut squash and/or rutabaga, peeled, seeded, and sliced (about 6 cups)
- ½ cup reduced-sodium beef broth
- ½ cup dry red wine
- 2 Tbsp. soy sauce
- 4 cloves garlic, minced
- 1 tsp. dried thyme, crushed
- 2 Tbsp. tomato paste
- 2 Tbsp. prepared horseradish
  Hot cooked noodles
  Fresh thyme

FAST *30-MINUTE COOK TIME*

Season ribs with paprika, salt, and pepper. In a 6-qt. electric pressure cooker use the saute setting to cook ribs, half at a time, in hot oil until browned on all sides. For a stove-top cooker, cook directly in pot over medium-high heat. Add squash, broth, wine, soy sauce, garlic, and dried thyme. Lock lid in place. Set an electric cooker on high pressure to cook 30 minutes. For a stove-top cooker, bring up to pressure over medium-high heat; reduce heat enough to maintain steady pressure. Cook 30 minutes. Remove from heat.

For both models, let stand 15 minutes to release pressure naturally. Carefully open lid. Transfer ribs and vegetables to serving dish. Skim fat from cooking liquid. Whisk in tomato paste and horseradish. Serve sauce with ribs and noodles. Top with fresh thyme.

SLOW *10-HOUR LOW OR 5-HOUR HIGH COOK TIME*

Season ribs with paprika, salt, and pepper. In an extra-large skillet cook meat in hot oil over medium-high heat until browned, turning occasionally. Transfer to a 6-qt. slow cooker. Add squash, broth, wine, soy sauce, garlic, and dried thyme. Cover and cook on low 10 to 12 hours or high 5 to 6 hours.

Transfer ribs and vegetables to a serving dish. Skim fat from cooking liquid. Whisk in tomato paste and horseradish. Serve sauce with ribs and noodles. Top with fresh thyme.

PER SERVING 684 cal., 43 g fat (18 g sat. fat), 159 mg chol., 773 mg sodium, 30 g carb., 3 g fiber, 4 g sugars, 42 g pro.

RED WINE POT ROAST

Makes 6 servings

- 1   2- to 2½-lb. boneless beef chuck pot roast, trimmed
- 2   Tbsp. olive oil
- 2   cloves garlic, minced
- ¾   cup dry red wine
- 2   Tbsp. tomato paste
- ¾   cup 50%-less-sodium beef broth
- ½   tsp. salt
- ½   tsp. black pepper
- 1   tsp. dried thyme, crushed
- 2   Tbsp. quick-cooking tapioca, crushed (slow cooker only)
- 1   lb. tiny new red potatoes
- 4   large carrots, cut into 1½-inch pieces
- 2   cups 1-inch pieces peeled rutabaga
- 1   cup 1-inch pieces celery
- 2   Tbsp. cornstarch (pressure cooker only)

FAST   *40-MINUTE COOK TIME*

In a 6-qt. electric pressure cooker use the saute setting to cook meat in hot oil until browned on all sides. For a stove-top pressure cooker, cook meat directly in the pot over medium-high heat. Remove meat. Add garlic to pot; cook 1 minute, stirring constantly. Carefully add wine to pot, stirring to scrape up any browned bits. Stir in tomato paste, broth, salt, pepper, and thyme. Return meat to pot; add potatoes, carrots, rutabaga, and celery. Lock lid in place. Set an electric cooker on high pressure to cook 40 minutes. For a stove-top cooker, bring up to pressure over medium-high heat; reduce heat enough to maintain steady pressure. Cook 40 minutes. Remove from heat.

For both models, let stand 15 minutes to release pressure naturally. Release any remaining pressure. Carefully open lid. Using a slotted spoon, transfer meat and vegetables to a platter. Skim fat from cooking liquid. In a small bowl combine 2 Tbsp. each cornstarch and cold water; stir into cooking liquid. For an electric cooker, heat to simmering on saute setting. For a stove-top cooker, bring to simmering over medium heat. Cook and stir until thickened and bubbly. Season to taste with additional salt and pepper. Serve cooking liquid with meat and vegetables.

SLOW   *10-HOUR LOW OR 5-HOUR HIGH COOK TIME*

In a large skillet cook meat in hot oil over medium-high heat until browned on all sides. Transfer meat to a 6-qt. slow cooker. In the same skillet cook garlic 1 minute, stirring constantly. Carefully add wine to skillet, stirring to scrape up any browned bits. Stir in tomato paste, broth, salt, pepper, thyme, and tapioca. Add potatoes, carrots, rutabaga, and celery to cooker.

Cover and cook on low 10 to 11 hours or high 5 to 5½ hours. Using a slotted spoon, transfer meat and vegetables to a platter. Season to taste with additional salt and pepper. Skim fat from cooking liquid; serve with meat and vegetables.

PER SERVING *382 cal., 11 g fat (3 g sat. fat), 98 mg chol., 471 mg sodium, 27 g carb., 5 g fiber, 7 g sugars, 37 g pro.*

STROGANOFF-STYLE POT ROAST

Makes 6 servings

- 1 2½ lb. beef chuck or arm roast
- 1 Tbsp. vegetable oil
- 8 oz. button mushrooms, quartered
- 1 cup thinly sliced onion
- 2 tsp. Dijon-style mustard
- 2 cloves garlic, minced
- 1 tsp. black pepper
- 1 cup beef broth
- 1 8-oz. carton sour cream
- 2 Tbsp. all-purpose flour

  Mashed potatoes or cooked noodles

  Snipped fresh chives

  Cracked black pepper

FAST *45-MINUTE COOK TIME*

In a 6-qt. electric pressure cooker use the saute setting to cook beef in hot oil until browned on both sides. For a stove-top cooker, cook directly in the pot over medium-high heat. Add mushrooms, onion, mustard, garlic, and pepper. Pour broth over all. Lock lid in place. Set an electric cooker on high pressure to cook 45 minutes. For a stove-top cooker, bring up to pressure over medium-high heat. Cook 45 minutes. Remove from heat.

For both models, let stand 15 minutes to release pressure naturally. Release any remaining pressure. Carefully open lid. Transfer roast to a platter; let rest 10 minutes before pulling into serving, size pieces. For gravy, in a small bowl stir together sour cream and flour. Add to liquid in pot. Bring just to boiling, stirring until thickened. Pull meat into serving-size pieces and serve on mashed potatoes with gravy. Top with chives and cracked black pepper.

SLOW *8-HOUR LOW OR 4-HOUR HIGH COOK TIME + 30 MINUTES HIGH*

In a large skillet cook beef in hot oil until browned on both sides. Transfer to a 3½- or 4-qt. slow cooker. Add mushrooms, onion, mustard, garlic, and pepper. Pour broth over all. Cover and cook on low 8 to 10 hours or high 4 to 5 hours. Transfer roast to a platter; cover to keep warm. If using low, turn to high.

For gravy, in a bowl stir together sour cream and flour. Add to liquid in slow cooker. Cook, covered, 30 minutes or until thickened. Pull meat into serving-size pieces and serve on mashed potatoes with gravy. Top with chives and cracked black pepper.

PER SERVING *488 cal., 19 g fat (7 g sat. fat), 168 mg chol., 336 mg sodium, 28 g carb., 2 g fiber, 4 g sugars, 49 g pro.*

GERMAN BEEF ROULADES

Makes 4 servings

- 1¼ to 1½ lb. beef round steak, trimmed
- ¼ tsp. salt
- ¼ tsp. black pepper
- ¼ cup stone-ground mustard
- 2 slices bacon, cut in half crosswise
- 2 dill pickle spears, halved lengthwise
- 1 Tbsp. olive oil
- 1 14.5-oz. can reduced-sodium beef broth
- 1 bay leaf
- ¼ cup all-purpose flour
- 2 Tbsp. water
- 2 Tbsp. Worcestershire sauce
- ½ tsp. dried thyme, crushed
- Hot cooked spaetzle or noodles
- Chopped fresh Italian parsley

DIRECTIONS

Cut steak into four pieces. Place each piece between plastic wrap. Using the flat side of a meat mallet, pound meat to about ¼-inch thickness (about 5 inches wide). Season both sides with salt and pepper. Spread each piece with 1 Tbsp. of the mustard. Place one bacon piece and one pickle spear half in the center lengthwise. Fold together long sides of steak to enclose pickle; secure with toothpicks (some pickle may be exposed). Prepare as directed for desired cooker, below.

FAST *20-MINUTE COOK TIME*

In a 6-qt. electric pressure cooker use the saute setting to cook roulades in hot oil 4 to 5 minutes or until browned on all sides. For a stove-top cooker, cook directly in pot over medium-high heat. Add broth and bay leaf. Lock lid in place. Set an electric cooker on high pressure to cook 20 minutes. For a stove-top cooker, bring up to pressure over medium-high heat; reduce heat enough to maintain steady pressure. Cook 20 minutes. Remove from heat.

For both models, let stand 15 minutes to release pressure naturally. Release any remaining pressure. Carefully open lid. Transfer roulades to a platter; cover to keep warm. Remove and discard bay leaf.

In a bowl stir together flour, the water, Worcestershire sauce, and thyme. Add to cooking liquid in pot. Cook and stir over medium heat until thickened and bubbly. Cook and stir 1 minute more. Serve roulades over spaetzle and top with sauce. Sprinkle with parsley.

SLOW *4-HOUR HIGH COOK TIME*

In a large skillet heat oil over medium-high heat. Cook roulades 4 to 5 minutes until browned on all sides. Place roulades in a 4-qt. slow cooker. Add broth and bay leaf. Cover and cook on high 4 hours.

Transfer roulades to a platter; cover to keep warm. Pour cooking liquid into a medium saucepan; remove and discard bay leaf. In a bowl stir together flour, the water, Worcestershire sauce, and thyme. Add to cooking liquid. Cook and stir over medium heat until thickened and bubbly. Cook and stir 1 minute more. Serve roulades over spaetzle and top with sauce. Sprinkle with parsley.

PER SERVING 499 cal., 125 g fat (8 g sat. fat), 133 mg chol., 968 mg sodium, 29 g carb., 1 g fiber, 2 g sugars, 36 g pro.

GREEN CHILE PORK

[WEEKNIGHT] --- [COMPANY]

Makes 12 servings

- 1 3- to 3½-lb. boneless pork shoulder roast, trimmed and cut into 2-inch pieces
- 2 Tbsp. vegetable oil
- 2 fresh poblano chile peppers, seeded and chopped (tip p. 42)
- 1 cup chopped onion
- 1 cup salsa verde
- 1 4-oz. can diced green chile peppers, undrained
- 1 Tbsp. chili powder
- 2 tsp. ground cumin
- 1 tsp. ground coriander
- 1 tsp. dried oregano, crushed
- ¼ tsp. salt
- ¼ tsp. black pepper

FAST   45-MINUTE COOK TIME

In a 6-qt. electric pressure cooker use the saute setting to cook meat in hot oil until browned. For a stove-top cooker, cook meat directly in the pot over medium-high heat. Add poblano peppers and onion. Stir in remaining ingredients. Lock lid in place. Set an electric cooker on high pressure to cook 45 minutes. For a stove-top cooker, bring up to pressure over medium-high heat; reduce heat enough to maintain steady pressure. Cook 45 minutes. Remove from heat.

For both models, let stand 15 minutes to release pressure naturally. Release any remaining pressure. Carefully open lid. Using a slotted spoon, transfer pork to a serving bowl. Shred meat using two forks. Skim fat from cooking liquid. Stir enough cooking liquid into chile pork to moisten.

SLOW   8-HOUR LOW OR 4-HOUR HIGH COOK TIME

In a large skillet heat oil over medium-high heat. Add meat, one-third at a time, and cook until browned. Transfer meat to a 5- to 6-qt. slow cooker. Add poblano peppers and onion. In a small bowl combine remaining ingredients; pour over mixture in cooker. Cover and cook on low 8 to 10 hours or high 4 to 5 hours.

Using a slotted spoon, transfer pork to a serving bowl. Shred meat using two forks. Skim fat from cooking liquid. Stir enough cooking liquid into chile pork to moisten.

LEFTOVERS?

Serve this savory meat in tacos, burrito bowls, and pork sandwiches; on nachos or baked potatoes; or stuffed in pita pockets. Freeze in an airtight container up to 3 months. Thaw 8 hours in the refrigerator.

PER SERVING *252 cal., 16 g fat (5 g sat. fat), 70 mg chol., 285 mg sodium, 5 g carb., 1 g fiber, 2 g sugars, 21 g pro.*

PORK ROAST AND ROOTS
WITH QUICK APRICOT SAUCE

[WEEKNIGHT]---[HEALTHY]---[COMPANY]--

Makes 6 servings

- 1 medium fennel bulb (tip p 213)
- 2 medium parsnips, peeled
- 3 medium carrots, peeled
- 2 to 2½ lb. boneless pork shoulder roast
- 2 tsp. paprika
- 1 tsp. ground coriander
- ½ tsp. salt
- ½ tsp. black pepper
- 1 Tbsp. vegetable oil
- ¾ cup water
- 1 12-oz. jar apricot or peach preserves
- 3 Tbsp. white balsamic vinegar
- 1 Tbsp. snipped fresh sage

DIRECTIONS

Trim stalks from fennel bulb. Reserve some feathery tops (fronds) for garnish. Cut a thin slice from base of bulb; cut bulb in half. Remove and discard core. Cut bulb into 1-inch wedges; set aside. Cut parsnips crosswise in half. Cut thick ends lengthwise in half. Cut all portions crosswise into 2-inch lengths; set aside. Cut carrots crosswise into 2- to 3-inch lengths; set aside. Prepare as directed for desired cooker, below.

FAST 55-MINUTE COOK TIME

Cut meat into 3 or 4 equal portions; trim fat. In a small bowl combine the next four ingredients (through pepper); sprinkle over meat. Preheat a 6-qt. electric pressure cooker using the saute setting or heat a 6-qt. stove-top pressure cooker over medium heat. Add oil and meat. Turn off cooker or remove from heat. Pour the ¾ cup water over meat in cooker. Set an electric cooker on high pressure to cook 45 minutes. For a stove-top cooker, bring up to pressure over medium-high heat; reduce heat enough to maintain steady pressure. Cook 45 minutes. Remove from heat. For both models, quickly release pressure. Add fennel wedges, parsnips, and carrots to pot. Lock lid in place. Set an electric cooker on high pressure to cook 10 minutes. For a stove-top cooker, bring up to pressure over medium-high heat; reduce heat enough to maintain steady pressure. Cook 10 minutes. Remove from heat. Quickly release pressure. In a small saucepan combine preserves and vinegar. Simmer until preserves are melted, snipping any large fruit pieces. Stir in sage. Transfer meat and vegetables to a serving platter; top with fennel fronds. Serve with apricot sauce.

SLOW 9-HOUR LOW OR 4½-HOUR HIGH COOK TIME

Cut meat into 3 or 4 equal portions; trim fat. In a small bowl combine next four ingredients (through pepper); sprinkle over meat. In a large skillet cook meat, in batches if necessary, in hot oil over medium heat 6 to 8 minutes or until browned. Transfer meat to a 5- to 6-qt. slow cooker. Top with fennel wedges, parsnips, and carrots. Pour the water over all. Cover and cook on low 9 to 10 hours or high 4½ to 5 hours.

In a small saucepan combine preserves and vinegar. Simmer until preserves are melted, snipping any large fruit pieces. Stir in sage. Transfer meat and vegetables to a serving platter; top with fennel fronds. Serve with apricot sauce.

PER SERVING *370 cal., 8 g fat (2 g sat. fat), 61 mg chol., 24 mg sodium, 53 g carb., 4 g fiber, 35 g sugars, 21 g pro.*

ASIAN PORK CABBAGE BOWLS

Makes 6 servings

- 2 lb. pork shoulder, cut into 1½-inch pieces
- ¼ tsp. salt
- ¼ tsp. black pepper
- 1 Tbsp. vegetable oil
- 1 cup reduced-sodium chicken broth
- 1 8-oz. pkg. button mushrooms, quartered
- 1 Tbsp. sliced fresh ginger
- 1 Tbsp. reduced-sodium soy sauce
- 2 tsp. minced fresh lemongrass or lemongrass paste
- 3 cloves garlic, sliced
- ½ head napa cabbage, shredded (6 to 7 cups)
- 1½ cups coarsely shredded carrots
- 1 10-oz. pkg. frozen shelled edamame, cooked according to package directions
- ¾ cup thinly sliced red onion
- Bottled Asian salad dressing
- Chopped salted roasted peanuts
- Sriracha sauce (optional)

FAST   20-MINUTE COOK TIME

Season pork with salt and pepper. in a 6-qt. electric pressure cooker use the saute setting to cook pork in hot oil until browned on all sides. For a stove-top cooker, cook directly in the pot over medium-high heat. Add the next six ingredients (through garlic). Lock lid in place. Set an electric cooker on high pressure to cook 20 minutes. For a stove-top cooker, bring up to pressure over medium-high heat; reduce heat enough to maintain steady pressure. Cook 20 minutes. Remove from heat.

For both models, let stand 15 minutes to release pressure naturally. Release any remaining pressure. Carefully open lid. Using a slotted spoon, transfer pork and mushrooms to a bowl; shred pork with two forks. Skim fat from cooking liquid. Add enough reserved cooking liquid to moisten pork. Divide cabbage among six bowls. Top with carrots, edamame, red onion, pork, and mushrooms. Drizzle with Asian salad dressing. Sprinkle with chopped peanuts. If desired, serve with sriracha sauce.

SLOW   8-HOUR LOW OR 4-HOUR HIGH COOK TIME

Season pork with salt and pepper. In a large skillet heat oil over medium-high heat. Add pork; cook until browned on all sides. Transfer pork and juices to a 4-qt. slow cooker. Add the next six ingredients (through garlic). Cover and cook on low 8 to 9 hours or high 4 to 5 hours or until pork is fork-tender. Using a slotted spoon, transfer pork and mushrooms to a bowl; shred pork with two forks. Skim fat from cooking liquid. Add enough reserved cooking liquid to moisten pork. Divide cabbage among six bowls. Top with carrots, edamame, red onion, pork, and mushrooms. Drizzle with Asian salad dressing. Sprinkle with chopped peanuts. If desired, serve with sriracha sauce.

PREPPING LEMONGRASS

To slice fresh lemongrass, cut off the lower bulb; remove tough outer leaves, leaving a yellow stalk. Cut the stalk into thin slices. Place slices in a food processor and pulse until minced.

PER SERVING *399 cal., 21 g fat (4 g sat. fat), 61 mg chol., 771 mg sodium, 22 g carb., 5 g fiber, 11 g sugars, 31 g pro.*

LOIN BACK RIBS WITH
APPLE-SHALLOT MAPLE GLAZE

Makes 8 servings

- 3½ to 4 lb. pork loin back ribs, trimmed
- 2 tsp. ground ginger
- 2 tsp. onion powder
- 1 tsp. salt
- 1 tsp. ground mustard
- 1 tsp. black pepper
- ¾ cup water
- 1 recipe Apple-Shallot Maple Glaze

DIRECTIONS

Cut ribs into two-rib portions. In a bowl combine the next five ingredients (through pepper). Sprinkle seasoning over ribs; rub in with your fingers. Prepare as directed for desired cooker, below.

FAST *25-MINUTE COOK TIME*

Place seasoned ribs in a 6-qt. electric or stove-top pressure cooker. Add the water. Set an electric cooker on high pressure to cook 25 minutes. For a stove-top cooker, bring up to pressure over medium-high heat; reduce heat enough to maintain steady pressure. Cook 25 minutes. Remove from heat.

For both models, let stand 15 minutes to release pressure naturally. Release any remaining pressure. Carefully open lid. Preheat broiler. Line a large shallow baking pan with foil. Place ribs in a single layer in pan. Brush ribs with some of the Apple-Shallot Maple Glaze. Broil 5 to 6 inches from heat 4 to 6 minutes or until glaze just starts to brown, brushing with additional glaze halfway through broiling. Serve ribs with remaining glaze.

SLOW *6-HOUR LOW OR 3-HOUR HIGH COOK TIME*

Place seasoned ribs in a 5- to 6-qt. slow cooker. Add the water. Cover and cook on low 6 to 7 hours or high 3 to 3½ hours.

Preheat broiler. Line a large shallow baking pan with foil. Place ribs in a single layer in pan. Brush ribs with some of the Apple-Shallot Maple Glaze. Broil 5 to 6 inches from heat 4 to 6 minutes or until glaze just starts to brown, brushing with additional glaze halfway through broiling. Serve ribs with remaining glaze.

APPLE-SHALLOT MAPLE GLAZE
In a saucepan cook ⅓ cup finely chopped shallots in 2 Tbsp. hot oil over medium-low heat 5 minutes or until tender, stirring occasionally. Whisk in 1¾ cups apple juice, one 6-oz. can tomato paste, ½ cup pure maple syrup, ¼ cup apple cider vinegar, and 2 Tbsp. spicy brown mustard. Add 1 sprig fresh rosemary. Bring to boiling, stirring frequently. Reduce heat. Simmer, uncovered, 15 minutes or until sauce is thickened. Remove from heat. Cool slightly; remove and discard rosemary.

PER SERVING *274 cal, 11 g fat (4 g sat. fat), 65 mg chol., 622 mg sodium, 21 g carb, 1 g fiber, 17 g sugars, 22 g pro.*

TANGY MOLASSES
BARBECUE RIBS

Makes 8 servings

- 2 Tbsp. packed brown sugar
- 1 tsp. kosher salt
- 1 tsp. dry mustard
- 1 tsp. smoked paprika
- ½ tsp. garlic salt
- ½ tsp. black pepper
- 1 recipe Zingy Barbecue Sauce or 2 cups purchased barbecue sauce
- 6 to 7 lb. pork loin back ribs, trimmed and cut into 3- to 4-rib portions
- ½ cup beef broth
- 2 tsp. liquid smoke (optional)

DIRECTIONS

For rub, in a small bowl stir together the first six ingredients (through pepper). Sprinkle mixture over ribs; rub in with your fingers. Coat ribs with half the Zingy Barbecue Sauce (chill remaining sauce until needed). Prepare as directed for desired cooker, below.

FAST   *30-MINUTE COOK TIME*

Place a steam basket in a 6-qt. electric or stove-top pressure cooker; add broth and, if desired, liquid smoke. Place seasoned ribs on steamer basket. Lock lid in place. Set an electric cooker on high pressure to cook 30 minutes. For a stove-top cooker, bring up to pressure over medium-high heat; reduce heat enough to maintain steady pressure. Cook 30 minutes. Remove from heat.

For both models, let stand 15 minutes to release pressure naturally. Release any remaining pressure. Carefully open lid. Preheat broiler. Line a baking sheet with foil. Transfer ribs to prepared baking sheet and coat with remaining sauce. Broil 4 to 5 inches from heat 3 to 5 minutes or until sauce is heated through.

SLOW   *9-HOUR LOW OR 4½-HOUR HIGH COOK TIME*

In a 6-qt. slow cooker combine broth and, if desired, liquid smoke. Add seasoned ribs to cooker. Cover and cook on low 9 to 10 hours or high 4½ to 5 hours or until ribs are tender.

Preheat broiler. Line a baking sheet with foil. Transfer ribs to prepared baking sheet and coat with remaining sauce. Broil 4 to 5 inches from heat 3 to 5 minutes or until sauce is heated through.

ZINGY BARBECUE SAUCE

In a small bowl combine 1¼ cups ketchup, ¼ cup mild-flavor molasses, 3 Tbsp. Dijon-style mustard, and 1 Tbsp. each packed brown sugar, smoked paprika, cider vinegar, and Worcestershire sauce. Store in refrigerator up to 1 month. Makes 2 cups.

PER SERVING *562 cal., 32 g fat (12 g sat. fat), 146 mg chol., 888 mg sodium, 23 g carb., 0 g fiber, 21 g sugars, 41 g pro.*

LTRY

Chicken and turkey are so mildly flavored it's like having a blank canvas for adding flavor. Try global inspirations such as Indian Butter Chicken and Thai Turkey Meat Loaf, or fall back on comfort classics like chicken and noodles.

MOROCCAN APRICOT CHICKEN

Makes 8 servings

- ½ tsp. salt
- ½ tsp. ground ginger
- ½ tsp. ground turmeric
- ½ tsp. crushed red pepper
- ¼ tsp. ground allspice
- 8 bone-in chicken thighs and/or drumsticks (3 lb.), skinned
- 1 Tbsp. olive oil
- 2 medium onions, cut into wedges
- 6 large cloves garlic, halved lengthwise
- 1 lb. butternut squash, peeled, seeded, and cut into 1-inch cubes (3 cups)
- ¼ cup reduced-sodium chicken broth
- ½ cup snipped dried apricots or golden raisins
- 1 cup pitted Kalamata olives

  Hot cooked couscous or quinoa (optional)

  Lemon wedges (optional)

  Greek yogurt (optional)

  Snipped fresh Italian parsley (optional)

DIRECTIONS

In a small bowl combine the first five ingredients (through allspice). Sprinkle spice mixture over chicken; rub in with your fingers. Prepare as directed for desired cooker, below.

FAST *8-MINUTE COOK TIME*

In a 6-qt. electric pressure cooker use the saute setting to heat 2 tsp. of the oil. Cook seasoned chicken, in batches, 6 to 8 minutes or until browned on all sides. For a stove-top cooker, cook directly in the pot over medium heat. Remove chicken from pot. Add 1 tsp. of the olive oil to pot. Add onions and garlic; cook 2 minutes. Add squash; toss lightly. Add chicken and broth. Lock lid in place. Set an electric cooker on high pressure to cook 8 minutes. For a stove-top cooker, bring up to pressure over medium-high heat; reduce heat enough to maintain steady pressure. Cook 8 minutes. Remove from heat.

For both models, let stand 15 minutes to release pressure naturally. Release any remaining pressure. Carefully open lid. Stir in apricots and olives. If desired, serve over hot cooked couscous or quinoa with lemon wedges, yogurt, and/or parsley.

SLOW *4-HOUR LOW OR 2-HOUR HIGH COOK TIME*

In an extra-large skillet heat oil over medium heat. Add seasoned chicken; cook 6 to 8 minutes or until browned on all sides. In a 5- to 6-qt. slow cooker combine onions, garlic, and squash. Add chicken. Stir broth into drippings in skillet; add to cooker. Cover and cook on low 4 to 6 hours or high 2 to 3 hours. Stir in apricots and olives. If desired, serve over hot cooked couscous or quinoa with lemon wedges, yogurt, and/or parsley.

TIME-SAVER

Cut prep time by using frozen cubed butternut squash in place of the fresh. Freezing makes the squash softer but the texture will be fine.

PER SERVING *212 cal., 9 g fat (1 g sat. fat), 60 mg chol., 619 mg sodium, 16 g carb., 2 g fiber, 7 g sugars, 17 g pro.*

INDIAN BUTTER CHICKEN

Makes 6 servings

- 6 Tbsp. butter
- 1¾ lb. skinless, boneless chicken thighs
- 1 Tbsp. grated fresh ginger
- 1 Tbsp. garam masala
- 3 cloves garlic, minced
- 1 tsp. ground cumin
- ½ tsp. salt
- ½ tsp. ground turmeric
- ¼ tsp. cayenne pepper
- 1 14.5-oz. can diced tomatoes, undrained
- 1 cup chopped onion
- ½ cup heavy cream
  Hot cooked basmati rice
  Chopped fresh cilantro
- 6 naan, warmed (optional)

FAST *5-MINUTE COOK TIME*

In a 6-qt. electric pressure cooker use the saute setting to heat 3 Tbsp. of the butter. Add chicken; cook 4 minutes or until lightly browned, turning once. For a stove-top cooker, cook directly in the pot over medium heat. Add the next nine ingredients (through onion). Lock lid in place. Set an electric cooker on high pressure to cook 5 minutes. For a stove-top cooker, bring up to pressure over medium-high heat; reduce heat enough to maintain steady pressure. Cook 5 minutes. Remove from heat.

For both models, let stand 15 minutes to release pressure naturally. Release any remaining pressure. Carefully open lid. Stir in cream and remaining 3 Tbsp. butter. Serve over rice. Sprinkle with cilantro. If desired, serve with warm naan.

SLOW *6-HOUR LOW OR 3-HOUR HIGH COOK TIME*

In a large skillet heat 3 Tbsp. of the butter over medium heat. Add chicken; cook 4 minutes or until lightly browned, turning once. Transfer chicken to a 3½- or 4-qt. slow cooker. Add the next seven ingredients (through cayenne pepper); toss to coat. Stir in tomatoes and onion. Cover and cook on low 6 hours or high 3 hours. Stir in cream and remaining 3 Tbsp. butter. Serve over rice. Sprinkle with cilantro. If desired, serve with warm naan.

NAAN VS. PITA

Both lightly leavened, soft Indian naan is blistered quickly in a hot clay oven and contains dairy. Middle Eastern pita is a drier oven-baked bread that, when split, reveals a pocket for filling.

PER SERVING *467 cal., 24 g fat (13 g sat. fat), 177 mg chol., 1,014 mg sodium, 31 g carb., 2 g fiber, 3 g sugars, 30 g pro.*

MUSHU-STYLE CHICKEN

Makes 6 servings

- ½ cup hoisin sauce
- 2 Tbsp. water
- 4 tsp. toasted sesame oil
- 1 Tbsp. cornstarch
- 1 Tbsp. reduced-sodium soy sauce
- 3 large cloves garlic, minced
- 1 14- to 16-oz. pkg. shredded cabbage with carrots (coleslaw mix)
- 1 cup coarsely shredded carrots
- 12 oz. skinless, boneless chicken thighs, thinly sliced
- 6 8-inch warm flour tortillas

  Sliced green onions

DIRECTIONS

For sauce, in a small bowl combine the first six ingredients (through garlic). Prepare as directed for desired cooker, below.

FAST *5-MINUTE COOK TIME*

In a 6-qt. electric or stove-top pressure cooker combine coleslaw mix, shredded carrots, and ¼ cup water. Place chicken on cabbage mixture. Drizzle with ¼ cup of the sauce. Lock lid in place. Set an electric cooker on high pressure to cook 5 minutes. For a stove-top cooker, bring up to pressure over medium-high heat; reduce heat enough to maintain steady pressure. Cook 5 minutes. Remove from heat.

For both models, let stand 15 minutes to release pressure naturally. Release any remaining pressure. Carefully open lid. Using a slotted spoon, spoon chicken mixture on tortillas (discard cooking liquid). Drizzle with remaining sauce. Top with green onions.

SLOW *6-HOUR LOW OR 3-HOUR HIGH COOK TIME*

In a 3½- or 4-qt. slow cooker combine coleslaw mix and shredded carrots. Place chicken on cabbage mixture. Drizzle with ¼ cup of the sauce. Cover and cook on low 6 hours or high 3 hours. Using a slotted spoon, spoon chicken mixture on tortillas (discard cooking liquid). Drizzle with remaining sauce. Top with green onions.

PER SERVING *321 cal., 10 g fat (2 g sat. fat), 54 mg chol., 874 mg sodium, 39 g carb., 4 g fiber, 10 g sugars, 14 g pro.*

SIMPLIFIED CHICKEN KORMA

[HEALTHY]---[COMPANY]--

Makes 10 servings

- 3 lb. skinless, boneless chicken thighs, cut into 1½-inch pieces
- 2 medium sweet potatoes, cut into 2-inch pieces
- 1½ cups thinly sliced onion
- 3 cloves garlic, minced
- 1 14-oz. can unsweetened coconut milk
- 2 Tbsp. tomato paste
- 1 Tbsp. grated fresh ginger
- 1 Tbsp. garam masala
- 2 tsp. ground turmeric
- 2 tsp. chili powder
- 1 tsp. salt
- ⅓ cup ground almonds or almond meal
- ¼ cup plain Greek yogurt
- Hot cooked basmati or long grain white rice

FAST *10-MINUTE COOK TIME*

In a 6-qt. electric or stove-top pressure cooker combine the first 11 ingredients (through salt). Lock lid in place. Set an electric cooker on high pressure to cook 10 minutes. For a stove-top cooker, bring up to pressure over medium-high heat; reduce heat enough to maintain steady pressure. Cook 10 minutes. Remove from heat.

For both models, let stand 15 minutes to release pressure naturally. Release any remaining pressure. Carefully open lid. Stir in ground almonds and yogurt. Serve over rice.

SLOW *7-HOUR LOW OR 3½-HOUR HIGH COOK TIME*

In a 3½- or 4-qt. slow cooker combine the first 11 ingredients (through salt). Cover and cook on low 7 to 8 hours or high 3½ to 4 hours. Stir in ground almonds and yogurt. Serve over rice.

GREAT GRATING

The easiest way to grate fresh ginger? Peel the ginger root, then wrap in plastic wrap and pop it in the freezer. When frozen, the fibers won't get stuck in your grater.

PER SERVING *414 cal., 14 g fat (8 g sat. fat), 128 mg chol., 701 mg sodium, 38 g carb., 3 g fiber, 4 g sugars, 31 g pro.*

CHICKEN CACCIATORE

Makes 4 servings

- 8 skinless, boneless chicken thighs
- ½ tsp. salt
- ¼ tsp. black pepper
- 2 Tbsp. olive oil
- 1 cup chopped onion
- 1 8-oz. pkg. cremini mushrooms, sliced
- 2 cloves garlic, minced
- ½ cup dry white wine
- 1 28-oz. can stewed tomatoes, cut up (undrained)
- 1 medium yellow or red sweet pepper, halved, seeded, and sliced
- ½ tsp. dried rosemary, crushed
- ¼ tsp. crushed red pepper
- 4 cups hot cooked pasta
  Snipped fresh Italian parsley

FAST 8-MINUTE COOK TIME

Sprinkle chicken with ¼ tsp. of the salt and the black pepper. In a 6-qt. electric pressure cooker use the saute setting to cook chicken, half at a time, in 1 Tbsp. hot oil until browned on all sides. For a stove-top cooker, cook directly in the pot over medium-high heat. Remove chicken; drain off fat. Add remaining 1 Tbsp. oil to cooker. Add onion, mushrooms, and remaining ¼ tsp. salt; cook over medium-high heat 4 to 5 minutes or just until tender, stirring occasionally. Add garlic; cook and stir 30 seconds.

Turn off or remove from heat; carefully add wine. Return to heat; simmer 5 minutes. Add tomatoes, sweet pepper, rosemary, crushed red pepper, and chicken to cooker. Lock lid in place. Set an electric cooker on high pressure to cook 8 minutes. For a stove-top cooker, bring up to pressure over medium-high heat; reduce heat enough to maintain steady pressure. Cook 8 minutes. Remove from heat.

For both models, release pressure quickly. Carefully open lid. Serve chicken and vegetables with pasta. Sprinkle with parsley.

SLOW 5-HOUR LOW OR 2½-HOUR HIGH COOK TIME

Sprinkle chicken with ¼ tsp. of the salt and the black pepper. In an extra-large skillet cook chicken, half at a time, in 1 Tbsp. hot oil over medium-high heat until browned on all sides. Remove chicken; drain off fat. In the same skillet heat remaining 1 Tbsp. oil over medium-high heat. Add onion, mushrooms, and remaining ¼ tsp. salt; cook 4 to 5 minutes or just until tender, stirring occasionally. Add garlic; cook and stir 30 seconds.

Remove skillet from heat; carefully add wine. Return to heat; simmer 5 minutes. Transfer onion-mushroom mixture to a 5- to 6-qt. slow cooker. Add tomatoes, sweet pepper, rosemary, crushed red pepper, and chicken to cooker. Cover and cook on low 5 to 6 hours or high 2½ to 3 hours. Serve chicken and vegetables with pasta. Sprinkle with parsley.

PER SERVING *813 cal., 23 g fat (5 g sat. fat), 320 mg chol., 1,062 mg sodium, 66 g carb., 6 g fiber, 12 g sugars, 80 g pro.*

OLD-FASHIONED
CHICKEN AND NOODLES

Makes 8 servings

2	cups sliced carrots
1½	cups chopped onions
1½	cups sliced celery
2	cloves garlic, minced
1	tsp. dried thyme, crushed
1	bay leaf
½	tsp. salt
½	tsp. poultry seasoning
¼	tsp. black pepper
3	lb. meaty chicken pieces (drumsticks, thighs, and breast halves), skinned
4	cups reduced-sodium chicken broth
1	16-oz. pkg. frozen egg noodles
1½	cups frozen peas
2	Tbsp. lemon juice

FAST *8-MINUTE COOK TIME*

In a 6-qt. electric or stove-top pressure cooker place the first nine ingredients (through pepper). Top with chicken. Pour broth over all. Stir in uncooked frozen noodles. Lock lid in place. Set an electric cooker on high pressure to cook 8 minutes. For a stove-top cooker, bring up to pressure over medium-high heat; reduce heat enough to maintain steady pressure. Cook 8 minutes. Remove from heat.

For both models, let stand 15 minutes to release pressure naturally. Release any remaining pressure. Carefully open lid. Remove chicken; cool slightly. Remove and discard bay leaf. Remove chicken from bones. Chop chicken; return to cooker. Add peas and lemon juice. For an electric cooker, use the saute setting to heat through. For a stove-top cooker heat through over medium heat.

SLOW *8-HOUR LOW OR 4-HOUR HIGH COOK TIME*

In a 5- to 6-qt. slow cooker place the first nine ingredients (through pepper). Top with chicken. Pour broth over all. Cover and cook on low 8 to 9 hours or high 4 to 4½ hours. Remove chicken from cooker; cool slightly. Remove and discard bay leaf. Remove chicken from bones. Chop chicken; return to cooker.

Meanwhile, cook noodles according to package directions. Stir noodles, peas, and lemon juice into chicken mixture. Let stand 10 minutes to heat through.

UP the flavor

Stir in crushed red pepper, chili powder, taco seasoning, or curry powder.

PER SERVING *319 cal., 4 g fat (1 g sat. fat), 123 mg chol., 550 mg sodium, 41 g carb., 4 g fiber, 6 g sugars, 27 g pro.*

SRIRACHA-GINGER CHICKEN

Makes 6 servings

- 3 chicken breast halves with bone (about 1 lb. each), skinned
- ⅓ cup honey
- 3 Tbsp. sriracha sauce
- 2 Tbsp. rice vinegar
- 1 Tbsp. grated fresh ginger
- 3 cloves garlic, minced
- ½ tsp. toasted sesame oil
- 3 cups hot cooked brown rice
  Sliced green onions
  Coarsely chopped sriracha-flavor almonds or almonds

FAST *15-MINUTE COOK TIME*

Place chicken in a 6-qt. electric or stove-top pressure cooker. In a small bowl combine the next six ingredients (through sesame oil). Pour over chicken in cooker. Lock lid in place. Set an electric cooker on high pressure to cook 15 minutes. For a stove-top cooker, bring up to pressure over medium-high heat; reduce heat enough to maintain steady pressure. Cook 15 minutes. Remove from heat.

For both models, let stand 15 minutes to release pressure naturally. Release any remaining pressure. Carefully open lid. Transfer chicken mixture to a plate; cover to keep warm. For sauce, strain cooking liquid through a fine-mesh sieve into a bowl, then return to cooker. For an electric cooker use the saute setting to bring liquid to boiling; reduce heat. Simmer, uncovered, 10 to 12 minutes or until reduced by half. For a stove-top cooker, cook directly in the pot over medium heat. Remove bones from chicken; slice breasts crosswise. Serve chicken over rice. Drizzle with sauce; sprinkle with green onions and almonds.

SLOW *2½-HOUR HIGH COOK TIME*

Place chicken in a 3½- or 4-qt. slow cooker. In a small bowl combine the next six ingredients (through sesame oil). Pour over chicken in cooker. Cover and cook on high 2½ to 3 hours or until chicken is done (170°F). Transfer chicken mixture to a plate; cover to keep warm.

For sauce, strain cooking liquid through a fine-mesh sieve into a small saucepan. Bring to boiling; reduce heat. Simmer, uncovered, 10 to 12 minutes or until reduced by half. Remove bones from chicken; slice breasts crosswise. Serve chicken over rice. Drizzle with sauce; sprinkle with green onions and almonds.

PER SERVING *351 cal., 6 g fat (1 g sat. fat), 72 mg chol., 185 mg sodium, 41 g carb., 2 g fiber, 18 g sugars, 33 g pro.*

CHICKEN SHAWARMA

Makes 4 servings

- 1 cup shredded carrots
- ¼ cup finely chopped red onion
- ¼ cup unseasoned rice vinegar
- 2 tsp. sugar
  Salt and black pepper (optional)
- ½ cup plain yogurt
- 1 Tbsp. lemon juice
- ½ tsp. dried dill weed
- ½ tsp. honey
- 1¼ lb. skinless, boneless chicken thighs
- 1 Tbsp. ras el hanout
- 3 Tbsp. olive oil
- 1 cup reduced-sodium chicken broth
- 4 pita bread rounds, warmed

DIRECTIONS

For pickled carrots and red onion, in a small bowl combine carrots, onion, vinegar, and sugar. Season with salt and pepper, if desired. Cover and refrigerate until serving. For the lemon-yogurt sauce, in a small bowl whisk together yogurt, lemon juice, dill, and honey until smooth. Cover and refrigerate until serving. Prepare as directed for desired cooker, below.

FAST *15-MINUTE COOK TIME*

Rub chicken thighs with ras el hanout. Season with salt and pepper, if desired. In a 6-qt. electric pressure cooker use the saute setting cook chicken in hot oil 3 to 4 minutes or until browned. Turn; cook 2 minutes more. For a stove-top cooker, cook directly in the pot over medium-high heat. Add broth to pot. Lock lid in place. Set an electric cooker on high pressure to cook 15 minutes. For a stove-top cooker, bring up to pressure over medium-high heat; reduce heat enough to maintain steady pressure. Cook 15 minutes. Remove from heat.

For both models, let stand 15 minutes to release pressure naturally. Release any remaining pressure. Carefully open lid. Remove chicken from pot and slice. Discard broth. Spoon some lemon-yogurt sauce on pita bread rounds. Add chicken. Using a slotted spoon, top chicken with pickled carrots and red onion.

SLOW *2-HOUR HIGH COOK TIME*

Rub chicken thighs with ras el hanout. Season with salt and pepper, if desired. In a large nonstick skillet heat oil over medium-high heat. Add chicken; cook 3 to 4 minutes or until browned. Turn; cook 2 minutes more. Place chicken in a 3½- or 4-qt. slow cooker. Add broth. Cover and cook on high 2 hours or until done (170°F). Remove chicken from cooker and slice. Discard broth. Spoon some lemon-yogurt sauce on pita bread rounds. Add chicken. Using a slotted spoon, top chicken with pickled carrots and red onion.

*RAS EL HANOUT
This spice blend, common in North African and Moroccan cuisines, can consist of as many as 40 spices. Specialty and well-stocked grocers carry this popular spice blend; if you are unable to find it, follow this recipe: In a bowl combine 1 tsp. paprika, ½ tsp. ground cumin, ¼ tsp. ground cinnamon, ¼ tsp. ground coriander, ¼ tsp. ground ginger, ¼ tsp. black pepper, ¼ tsp. ground turmeric, and ⅛ tsp. cayenne pepper.

PER SERVING *485 cal., 18 g fat (3 g sat. fat), 135 mg chol., 776 mg sodium, 43 g carb., 2 g fiber, 8 g sugars, 36 g pro.*

ASIAN CHICKEN NOODLE BOWLS

Makes 6 servings

- 6 skinless, boneless chicken breast halves
- 1 cup reduced-sodium chicken broth
- 1 Tbsp. grated fresh ginger
- 1 Tbsp. Asian chili garlic sauce
- 1 Tbsp. soy sauce
- 2 cloves garlic, minced
- 12 oz. thin rice noodles
- ¼ cup fresh lime juice
- ¼ cup water
- 2 Tbsp. fish sauce
- 2 Tbsp. packed brown sugar
- 1 Tbsp. finely chopped, seeded red Fresno chile pepper or jalapeño pepper (tip p. 42)

Toppings

- 2 cups thinly sliced cucumbers
- ¾ cup shredded carrots
- ¼ cup fresh cilantro leaves
- 3 green onions, thinly sliced
- 3 Tbsp. shredded fresh Thai basil or basil leaves

FAST *5-MINUTE COOK TIME*

Place chicken in a 4- to 6-qt. electric or stove-top pressure cooker. Add the next five ingredients (through garlic). Lock lid in place. Set an electric cooker on high pressure to cook 5 minutes. For a stove-top cooker, bring up to pressure over medium-high heat; reduce heat enough to maintain steady pressure. Cook 5 minutes. Remove from heat.

For both models, release pressure quickly. Carefully open lid. Transfer chicken to a cutting board. Use two forks to shred chicken. Strain and reserve cooking liquid.

Meanwhile, prepare noodles according to package directions. Rinse with cold water; drain well. For sauce, in a small bowl combine lime juice, the water, fish sauce, sugar, and chile pepper. Divide noodles, chicken, and topping ingredients among bowls. Pour reserved liquid over bowls. Serve with sauce.

SLOW *4-HOUR LOW OR 2-HOUR HIGH COOK TIME*

Place chicken in a 3½- or 4-qt. slow cooker. Add the next five ingredients (through garlic). Cover and cook on low 4 hours or high 2 hours or until chicken is done (165°F). Transfer chicken to a cutting board. Use two forks to shred chicken. Strain and reserve cooking liquid.

Meanwhile, prepare noodles according to package directions. Rinse with cold water; drain well. For sauce, in a small bowl combine lime juice, the water, fish sauce, sugar, and chile pepper. Divide noodles, chicken, and topping ingredients among bowls. Pour reserved liquid over bowls. Serve with sauce.

TRY THAI BASIL

While sweet basil has anise flavor, Thai basil has even more intense anise flavor—a delicious companion to Southeast Asian food. Find this sturdy herb at local farmers markets or Asian food stores.

PER SERVING *529 cal., 6 g fat (1 g sat. fat), 165 mg chol., 982 mg sodium, 58 g carb., 2 g fiber, 8 g sugars, 57 g pro.*

CHICKEN AND SAUSAGE GUMBO

Makes 6 servings

- ½ cup all-purpose flour
- ½ cup vegetable oil
- 3 cups reduced-sodium chicken broth
- 1¼ lb. skinless, boneless chicken thighs, cut into 1½-inch pieces
- 1 12- to 14-oz. link andouille or kielbasa smoked sausage, sliced ½ inch thick
- ½ of a 10- to 12-oz. pkg. frozen cut okra, thawed
- ¾ cup chopped onion
- ¾ cup chopped green sweet pepper
- ¾ cup chopped celery
- 4 cloves garlic, minced
- 1 tsp. paprika
- ½ tsp. salt
- ½ tsp. black pepper
- ½ tsp. cayenne pepper
- 1 bay leaf
- ¼ cup thinly sliced green onions
  Hot cooked rice
- ¾ tsp. filé powder (optional)
  Sliced green onions (optional)
  Bottled hot pepper sauce (optional)

FAST *8-MINUTE COOK TIME*

For roux, in a 6-qt. electric pressure cooker stir together flour and oil until smooth. Use the saute setting to cook over medium heat 5 to 7 minutes or until roux is the color of peanut butter, stirring constantly. For a stove-top cooker, cook directly in the pot over medium heat. Carefully stir in broth. Add the next 12 ingredients (through bay leaf). Lock lid in place. Set an electric cooker on high pressure to cook 8 minutes. For a stove-top cooker, bring up to pressure over medium-high heat; reduce heat enough to maintain steady pressure. Cook 8 minutes. Remove from heat.

For both models, let stand 15 minutes to release pressure naturally. Release any remaining pressure. Carefully open lid. Remove and discard bay leaf. Skim off fat. Stir in green onions. Serve gumbo over rice. If desired, stir ⅛ tsp. filé powder into each serving. If desired, serve with additional green onions, and hot sauce.

SLOW *7-HOUR LOW OR 3½-HOUR HIGH COOK TIME*

For roux, in a medium-size heavy saucepan stir together flour and oil until smooth. Cook over medium heat 5 to 7 minutes until roux is the color of peanut butter, stirring constantly. Remove from heat. Place broth in a 5- to 6-qt. slow cooker. Carefully stir in the roux until well combined (it may pop and release steam). Add the next 12 ingredients (through bay leaf).

Cover and cook on low 7 to 8 hours or high 3½ to 4 hours. Remove and discard bay leaf. Skim off fat. Stir in green onions. Serve gumbo over rice. If desired, stir ⅛ tsp. filé powder into each serving. If desired, serve with additional green onions, and hot sauce.

FINDING FILÉ

Filé powder can be found in most well-stocked grocery stores and in specialty spice shops. This sassafras tree leaf powder acts as a thickener plus adds a distinctive, earthy flavor to gumbo.

PER SERVING *620 cal., 38 g fat (8 g sat. fat), 124 mg chol., 1,105 mg sodium, 38 g carb., 2 g fiber, 3 g sugars, 32 g pro.*

BOURBON BBQ
CHICKEN DRUMSTICKS

Makes 4 servings

- 1 cup ketchup
- ¼ cup packed brown sugar
- ¼ cup finely chopped onion
- 3 Tbsp. bourbon or apple juice
- 1 Tbsp. yellow mustard
- ½ tsp. crushed red pepper
- 2 Tbsp. packed brown sugar
- 2 tsp. onion powder
- 1 tsp. salt
- 1 tsp. garlic powder
- 1 tsp. chili powder
- ½ tsp. black pepper
- 8 chicken drumsticks, skinned, if desired

  Celery and carrot sticks (optional)

DIRECTIONS

For Bourbon BBQ Sauce, in a small saucepan combine the first six ingredients (through crushed red pepper). Bring to boiling; reduce heat. Simmer 5 minutes. Reserve about half the sauce for serving. For seasoning, in a small bowl combine the next six ingredients (through black pepper). Rub seasoning over drumsticks. Prepare as directed for desired cooker, below.

FAST *10-MINUTE COOK TIME*

Place drumsticks in a 6-qt. electric or stove-top pressure cooker. Drizzle remaining sauce over chicken, gently stirring to coat. Lock lid in place. Set an electric cooker on high pressure to cook 10 minutes. For a stove-top cooker, bring up to pressure over medium-high heat. Cook 10 minutes. Remove from heat.

For both models, quickly release pressure. Carefully open lid. Serve drumsticks with reserved Bourbon BBQ Sauce.

SLOW *5-HOUR LOW OR 2½-HOUR HIGH COOK TIME*

Place drumsticks in a 3½- or 4-qt. slow cooker. Drizzle remaining sauce over chicken, gently stirring to coat. Cover; cook on low 5 to 6 hours or high 2½ to 3 hours or until chicken is tender. Serve drumsticks with reserved Bourbon BBQ Sauce.

CRISP THE SKIN

For crisp chicken skin, transfer drumsticks from cooker to a foil-lined rimmed baking pan. Broil 4 inches from heat 2 to 3 minutes or until chicken is lightly browned, turning occasionally.

PER SERVING *414 cal., 14 g fat (4 g sat. fat), 134 mg chol., 1,348 mg sodium, 40 g carb., 1 g fiber, 33 g sugars, 28 g pro.*

DUCK BREAST WITH
MAPLE AND PLUMS

Makes 4 servings

4 boneless duck breasts with skin (about 1¾ lb.) or 8 bone-in chicken thighs (about 3 lb.)

½ tsp. kosher salt

¼ tsp. freshly ground black pepper

1 Tbsp. vegetable oil (if using chicken)

6 medium parsnips, peeled and cut into 2-inch chunks

4 shallots, halved or quartered (if large)

½ cup chicken broth

2 Tbsp. maple syrup

2 Tbsp. chopped fresh rosemary

2 cloves garlic, minced

4 fresh firm plums, pitted and halved

Fresh rosemary (optional)

DIRECTIONS

Score duck skin in a diamond pattern. Season duck or chicken with salt and pepper. Prepare as directed for desired cooker, below.

FAST *9-MINUTE COOK TIME*

In a 6-qt. electric pressure cooker use the saute setting to heat oil over medium-high heat (may omit oil for duck). Add duck or chicken, skin side down, and cook 3 minutes or until well-browned. For a stove-top cooker, cook directly in the pot over medium-high heat. Remove duck or chicken; set aside. Drain fat from cooker. Stir in the next six ingredients (through garlic). Place duck or chicken on top. Lock lid in place. Set an electric cooker on high pressure to cook 9 minutes for duck (10 minutes for chicken). For a stove-top cooker, bring up to pressure over medium-high heat; reduce heat enough to maintain steady pressure. Cook 9 minutes for duck (10 minutes for chicken). Remove from heat.

For both models, quickly release pressure. Carefully open lid. Using a slotted spoon, transfer duck or chicken and vegetables to a serving dish; cover to keep warm. Skim fat from cooking liquid and discard. For an electric cooker, use the saute setting to boil gently, uncovered, 15 minutes or until liquid is slightly syrupy, adding plums the last 5 minutes. For a stove-top cooker, cook directly in the pot over medium heat. Serve plums and sauce over duck or chicken and vegetables. If desired, top with fresh rosemary.

SLOW *5½-HOUR LOW OR 2¾-HOUR HIGH COOK TIME*

In a large skillet heat oil over medium-high heat (may omit oil for duck). Add duck or chicken, skin side down, and cook 3 minutes or until well-browned. In a 4-qt. oval slow cooker combine the next six ingredients (through garlic). (For chicken, use a 6-qt. slow cooker.) Place duck or chicken on top of vegetables. Cover; cook on low 5½ to 6½ hours or high 2¾ to 3¼ hours or until an instant-read thermometer inserted in duck registers 165°F (175°F for chicken thighs).

Using a slotted spoon, transfer duck or chicken and vegetables to a serving dish; cover to keep warm. Skim fat from cooking liquid and discard. Place cooking liquid in a medium saucepan; bring to boiling. Reduce heat; boil gently, uncovered, 15 minutes or until slightly syrupy, adding plums the last 5 minutes. Serve plums and sauce over duck or chicken and vegetables. If desired, top with fresh rosemary.

PER SERVING *581 cal., 26 g fat (6 g sat. fat), 270 mg chol., 428 mg sodium, 36 g carb., 7 g fiber, 19 g sugars, 51 g pro.*

THAI TURKEY MEAT LOAF

Makes 4 servings

- 1¼ lb. 93% lean ground turkey
- ½ cup chopped onion
- ½ cup shredded carrot
- ½ cup panko bread crumbs
- ¼ cup snipped fresh cilantro
- 1 jalapeño pepper, halved, seeded (if desired), and finely chopped (tip p. 42)
- 3 cloves garlic, minced
- 1 egg, lightly beaten
- 2 Tbsp. reduced-sodium soy sauce
- 2 Tbsp. grated fresh ginger
- 1 Tbsp. fish sauce
- ¼ tsp. black pepper
- ¼ cup Thai sweet chili sauce
- Fresh cilantro leaves

DIRECTIONS

In a large bowl combine the first 12 ingredients (through black pepper). Form into two 6×3-inch loaves. Prepare as directed for desired cooker, below.

FAST *15-MINUTE COOK TIME*

Place each loaf on a lightly greased 15×12-inch foil sheet. Wrap foil to completely enclose each loaf. Poke several holes in top of foil for steam to escape. Place a steam rack in a 6-qt. electric or stove-top pressure cooker. Add 1 cup water to pot. Place loaves on rack. Lock lid in place. Set an electric cooker on high pressure to cook 15 minutes. For a stove-top cooker, bring up to pressure over medium-high heat. Cook 15 minutes. Remove from heat.

For both models, let stand 10 minutes to release pressure naturally. Release any remaining pressure. Carefully open lid. Remove loaves from cooker. Unwrap loaves. Preheat broiler. Place loaves on a foil-lined baking sheet. Brush chili sauce over loaves. Broil 8 inches from heat 4 to 5 minutes or just until sauce starts to bubble. Top with cilantro leaves.

SLOW *5-HOUR LOW OR 2½-HOUR HIGH COOK TIME*

From heavy foil cut three 18×3-inch foil strips; fold in half lengthwise. Crisscross strips and place in a 3½- or 4-qt. oval slow cooker. Place loaves on foil strips. Fold strips inside pot. Cover and cook on low 5 to 6 hours or high 2½ to 3 hours or until a thermometer registers 165°F (meat may still look pink inside). Use foil strips to lift loaves from cooker. Preheat broiler. Line a baking sheet with foil. Place loaves on prepared baking sheet. Brush chili sauce over loaves. Broil 8 inches from heat 4 to 5 minutes or just until sauce starts to bubble. Top with cilantro leaves.

PER SERVING 318 cal., 13 g fat (3 g sat. fat), 151 mg chol., 1,024 mg sodium, 18 g carb., 1 g fiber, 11 g sugars, 30 g pro.

FISH &
FISH

SHELL

Delicate fish cooks fast in a pressure cooker (as quick as 1 minute!), while a slow cooker provides gentle heat to keep it moist.

SALMON WITH LENTIL HASH AND BACON

Makes 4 servings

- 2 cups reduced-sodium chicken broth
- 1 lb. baby yellow potatoes, halved
- 1 small head cauliflower (1½ lb.), cut into large florets
- 1 cup brown lentils, rinsed and drained
- 1 large onion, cut into quarters
- 4 cloves garlic, minced
- 1 Tbsp. curry powder
- ½ tsp. kosher salt
- ½ tsp. ground cumin
- ½ tsp. ground coriander
- ¼ tsp. cayenne pepper
- 1½ lb. salmon fillet, skinned
- Salt and black pepper
- 6 slices bacon, crisp-cooked and crumbled
- Fresh mint leaves

FAST *1-MINUTE COOK TIME*

In a 6-qt. electric or stove-top pressure cooker stir together the first 11 ingredients (through cayenne pepper). Cut salmon fillet in half crosswise; season with salt and black pepper. Place salmon on vegetables in cooker. Lock lid in place. Set an electric cooker on high pressure to cook 1 minute. For a stove-top cooker, bring up to pressure over medium-high heat; remove from heat.

For both models, release pressure quickly. Carefully open lid. Top servings with bacon and mint.

SLOW *5-HOUR LOW OR 2½-HOUR HIGH COOK TIME + 25 MINUTES HIGH*

In a 6-qt. slow cooker stir together the first 11 ingredients (through cayenne). Cover and cook on low 5 to 6 hours or high 2½ to 3 hours. If using low, turn to high. Cut salmon fillet in half crosswise; season with salt and black pepper. Place salmon on vegetables in cooker. Cover and cook 25 minutes more or just until salmon flakes. Top servings with bacon and mint.

PER SERVING 623 cal., 16 g fat (3 g sat. fat), 105 mg chol., 768 mg sodium, 63 g carb., 13 g fiber, 8 g sugars, 57 g pro.

GARLIC-GINGER SHRIMP WITH
COCONUT-CURRY VEGETABLES

Makes 4 servings

- 1 lb. fresh or frozen peeled and deveined jumbo shrimp (16/20 count)
- 1½ lb. peeled and seeded buttercup or butternut squash, cut into 2-inch cubes (4 cups)
- 4 medium parsnips or carrots, peeled, halved if large, and cut crosswise into ½-inch slices
- 1 cup canned coconut milk
- 2 Tbsp. red curry paste
- ¼ tsp. salt
- 1 Tbsp. finely chopped fresh ginger
- 3 cloves garlic, minced
- ¼ tsp. black pepper
- 1 cup diced fresh mango*
- ¼ cup unsweetened shredded coconut, lightly toasted (tip p. 20)
- ¼ cup snipped fresh cilantro

DIRECTIONS

Thaw shrimp, if frozen. Rinse shrimp and pat dry with paper towels; refrigerate until needed. prepare as directed for desired cooker, below.

FAST *6-MINUTE COOK TIME*

In a 6-qt. electric or stove-top pressure cooker combine squash and parsnips. In a medium bowl whisk together coconut milk, curry paste, and salt. Pour over vegetables in cooker. Lock lid in place. Set an electric cooker on high pressure to cook 2 minutes. For a stove-top cooker, bring up to pressure over medium-high heat; reduce heat enough to maintain steady pressure. Cook 2 minutes. Remove from heat.

For both models, release pressure quickly. Carefully open lid. In a large bowl toss together shrimp, ginger, garlic, and pepper. Arrange shrimp in an even layer over vegetables in cooker. Lock lid in place. Set an electric cooker on high pressure to cook 4 minutes. For a stove-top cooker, bring up to pressure over medium-high heat; reduce heat enough to maintain steady pressure. Cook 4 minutes. Remove from heat. For both models, release pressure quickly. Carefully open lid. Serve shrimp and vegetables with cooking juices; top with mango, coconut, and cilantro.

SLOW *3½-HOUR LOW OR 1¾-HIGH COOK TIME + 20 MINUTES HIGH*

In a 3½- or 4-qt. slow cooker combine squash and parsnips. In a medium bowl whisk together coconut milk, curry paste, and salt. Pour over vegetables in cooker. Cover and cook on low 3½ to 4 hours or on high 1¾ to 2 hours. In a large bowl toss together shrimp, ginger, garlic, and pepper. Arrange shrimp in an even layer over vegetables in cooker. If using low, turn to high. Cover and cook 20 to 30 minutes more or until shrimp are opaque.

STIR IT UP

Because coconut milk (in cans and cartons) tends to separate, shake the container well before opening, then thoroughly stir before measuring it to add to a recipe.

*INGREDIENT KNOW-HOW

Mangoes have a large, flat pit the length of the fruit. To cut a mango, set it on a narrow side and hold with one hand. Position a large sharp knife slightly off-center, then slice through the flesh. Repeat on the opposite side. Use a paring knife to score the flesh in a dice pattern up to, but not through, the skin. Press the flesh inside out and cut off the diced fruit.

PER SERVING *374 cal, 12 g fat (10 g sat. fat), 183 mg chol, 508 mg sodium, 42 g carb, 8 g fiber, 16 g sugars, 27 g pro.*

LOW-COUNTRY SHRIMP BOIL

Makes 12 servings

2 cups bottled clam juice

1 cup water

1 cup chopped onion

3 cloves garlic, minced

2 Tbsp. seafood seasoning (Old Bay)

1 lb. small red potatoes (1- to 1½-inch diameter), halved

12 to 16 oz. cooked kielbasa or other link sausage, cut into 2-inch pieces

4 ears fresh sweet corn, husks and silks removed, halved crosswise

1½ lb. fresh or frozen jumbo unpeeled shrimp (16/20 count), thawed

1 lemon

Melted butter

Lemon wedges

FAST *1-MINUTE COOK TIME*

In a 6-qt. electric or stove-top pressure cooker stir together the first five ingredients (through seasoning). Add potatoes, sausage, corn, and shrimp. Lock lid in place. Set an electric cooker on high pressure to cook 1 minute. For a stove-top cooker, bring up to pressure over medium-high heat; remove from heat.

For both models, release pressure quickly. Carefully open lid. Transfer potatoes, sausage, corn, and shrimp to a serving platter. Squeeze lemon over shrimp boil. Serve with melted butter and lemon wedges.

SLOW *4-HOUR HIGH COOK TIME*

In a 6-qt. slow cooker stir together the first seven ingredients (through kielbasa). Cover and cook on high 3 hours or until potatoes are nearly tender. Add corn and shrimp; cook 1 hour more or until corn is tender and shrimp are opaque. Transfer potatoes, sausage, corn, and shrimp to a serving platter. Squeeze lemon over shrimp boil. Serve with melted butter and lemon wedges.

PER SERVING *400 cal., 25 g fat (11 g sat. fat), 194 mg chol., 1,098 mg sodium, 23 g carb., 3 g fiber, 5 g sugars, 25 g pro.*

SIMPLIFIED PAELLA

Makes 4 servings

- 1 lb. medium fresh or frozen shrimp, peeled and deveined (16/20 count)
- 2 cups reduced-sodium chicken broth (pressure cooker only)
- 2½ cups reduced-sodium chicken broth (slow cooker only)
- 1 cup Arborio or long grain white rice (pressure cooker only)
- 1 cup uncooked converted rice (slow cooker only)
- 1 14.5-oz. can diced tomatoes, undrained
- ½ cup diced cooked andouille sausage
- 3 cloves garlic, sliced
- 1 bay leaf
- ¼ tsp. saffron threads, crushed (tip p. 274)
- ½ cup fresh or frozen peas
- ¼ cup dry white wine
- 2 Tbsp. lemon juice
- 8 oz. mussels in shells, scrubbed, beards removed,* and rinsed
- Crusty bread

DIRECTIONS

Thaw shrimp, if frozen. Rinse shrimp and pat dry with paper towels; refrigerate until needed. Prepare as directed for desired cooker, below.

FAST 10-MINUTE COOK TIME

In a 6-qt. electric or stove-top pressure cooker combine 2 cups broth, arborio rice, tomatoes, sausage, garlic, bay leaf, and saffron. Lock lid in place. Set an electric cooker on high pressure to cook 10 minutes. For a stove-top cooker, bring up to pressure over medium-high heat; reduce heat enough to maintain steady pressure. Cook 10 minutes. Remove from heat.

For both models, let stand 15 minutes to release pressure naturally. Release any remaining pressure. Carefully open lid. Stir in peas, wine, and lemon juice. Top with shrimp and mussels (do not stir in). Lock lid in place. Let stand 15 to 20 minutes or until mussels have opened and shrimp turn opaque. Remove and discard any unopened mussels. Serve in bowls with crusty bread.

SLOW 2-HOUR LOW COOK TIME + 1-HOUR HIGH

In a 4-qt. slow cooker combine 2 cups of the broth, the converted rice, tomatoes, sausage, garlic, bay leaf, and saffron. Cover and cook on low 2 hours or until rice is nearly tender. Stir in peas, wine, and lemon juice. Top with shrimp (do not stir). Increase heat to high. Cover and cook 1 hour more or until shrimp turn opaque.

In a large skillet bring remaining ½ cup broth to a simmer over medium heat. Add mussels to skillet. Cover and simmer 3 to 6 minutes or until mussels open. Discard any unopened mussels. Add to paella. Serve in bowls with crusty bread.

*DEBEARDING MUSSELS
Mussels have a collection of fibers that extend from their shells. These fibers, or byssal threads, are strong filaments formed by the mollusks to attach themselves to various surfaces in the sea. The beards are often removed during processing, but if you discover one still attached, grasp it between your thumb and forefinger and wriggle it back and forth while pulling it out. Scrub the shellfish with a food brush.

PER SERVING 535 cal., 8 g fat (2 g sat. fat), 202 mg chol., 1,254 mg sodium, 65 g carb., 3 g fiber, 4 g sugars, 45 g pro.

SEAFOOD CIOPPINO

Makes 8 servings

- 1 14.5-oz. can diced tomatoes, undrained
- 1 14.5-oz. can reduced-sodium chicken broth
- 2 medium red potatoes, chopped
- 1 medium onion, chopped
- 3 stalks celery, sliced
- 1 cup bottled clam juice
- 2 Tbsp. tomato paste
- 4 cloves garlic, minced
- 2 tsp. dried Italian seasoning, crushed
- 1 lb. halibut, sea bass, or other firm whitefish, cut in bite-size pieces
- 1 lb. uncooked shrimp, peeled and deveined (16/20 count)
- 1 6-oz. can lump crabmeat, drained
- ¼ cup dry white wine
- ¼ cup snipped fresh Italian parsley
  Kosher salt
  Toasted sourdough or French bread slices

FAST *1-MINUTE COOK TIME*

In a 6-qt. electric or stove-top pressure cooker combine the first nine ingredients (through Italian seasoning). Stir in fish, seafood, and wine. Lock lid in place. Set an electric cooker on high pressure 1 minute. For a stove-top cooker, bring up to pressure over medium-high heat; remove from heat.

For both models, let stand 5 minutes. Release pressure quickly. Carefully open lid. Stir in parsley. Season to taste with kosher salt. Serve with toasted bread.

SLOW *5-HOUR HIGH COOK TIME*

In a 5- to 6-qt. slow cooker combine the first nine ingredients (through Italian seasoning). Cover and cook on high 4½ to 5 hours. Stir in fish, seafood, and wine. Cook, covered, 30 minutes more or just until fish flakes and shrimp are opaque. Stir in parsley. Season to taste with kosher salt. Serve with toasted bread

PER SERVING *169 cal., 2 g fat (0 g sat. fat), 122 mg chol., 724 mg sodium, 13 g carb., 2 g fiber, 3 g sugars, 24 g pro.*

LEMONY MUSSELS WITH CHERRY TOMATOES AND POTATOES

Makes 4 servings

- 1 lb. tiny new red potatoes, halved
- 1 pint cherry tomatoes
- ½ cup vegetable broth or chicken broth
- ¼ cup dry white wine
- 1 shallot, finely chopped
- 4 cloves garlic, minced
- 1 tsp. dried oregano, crushed
- 1 bay leaf
- 1½ to 2 lb. mussels in shells, scrubbed, beards removed (tip p. 123), and rinsed
- 2 Tbsp. snipped fresh Italian parsley
- 2 Tbsp. butter
- 1 tsp. grated lemon zest
- 1 Tbsp. lemon juice
- Crusty bread

FAST *11-MINUTE COOK TIME*

In a 6-qt. electric or stove-top pressure cooker place potatoes and cherry tomatoes. Add the next six ingredients (through bay leaf). Lock lid in place. Set an electric cooker on high pressure to cook 6 minutes. For a stove-top cooker, bring up to pressure over medium-high heat; reduce heat enough to maintain steady pressure. Cook 6 minutes. Remove from heat.

For both models, let stand 6 minutes to release pressure naturally. Release any remaining pressure. Add mussels to cooker. Set an electric cooker on saute setting; cover (do not lock lid) and cook 5 to 7 minutes or until mussels open. For a stove-top cooker, cover (do not lock lid) and cook over medium-high heat 5 to 7 minutes or until mussels open. Discard any mussels that do not open. Remove and discard bay leaf. Add parsley, butter, lemon zest, and lemon juice; toss gently. Serve with crusty bread.

SLOW *6-HOUR LOW OR 3-HOUR HIGH COOK TIME + 45 MINUTES HIGH*

In a 5- to 6-qt. slow cooker place potatoes and cherry tomatoes. Add the next six ingredients (through bay leaf). Cover and cook on low 6 to 7 hours or high 3 to 3½ hours. If using low, turn to high. Add mussels. Cover and cook 45 minutes or until shells open. Discard any mussels that do not open. Remove and discard bay leaf. Add parsley, butter, lemon zest, and lemon juice; toss gently. Serve with crusty bread.

PER SERVING *329 cal, 10 g fat (5 g sat. fat), 66 mg chol., 674 mg sodium, 32 g carb., 4 g fiber, 5 g sugars, 25 g pro.*

CRAB-STUFFED PEPPERS

Makes 4 servings

- 4 small to medium red, yellow, and/or green sweet peppers
- 1 8-oz. pkg. cream cheese, softened
- 2 Tbsp. mayonnaise
- 2 Tbsp. lemon juice
- 1 Tbsp. seafood seasoning (Old Bay)
- 1 Tbsp. Dijon-style mustard
- ½ cup fine dry bread crumbs
- ⅓ cup finely chopped celery
- ¼ cup snipped fresh chives
- 4 cloves garlic, minced
- 8 oz. cooked lump crabmeat, flaked
  Freshly ground black pepper
  Lemon wedges

DIRECTIONS

Remove tops, seeds, and membranes from sweet peppers. If necessary, cut a thin slice from bottom of each peppers to stand upright (avoid cutting an opening). In a large bowl stir together the next five ingredients (through mustard) until smooth. Add next four ingredients (through garlic); stir until combined. Gently stir in crabmeat. Spoon crab filling into sweet peppers. Prepare as directed for desired cooker, below.

FAST *2-MINUTE COOK TIME*

Place a steam rack in a 6-qt. electric or stove-top pressure cooker. Add ¾ cup water to pot. Arrange peppers, filling sides up, on rack. Lock lid in place. Set an electric cooker on high pressure to cook 2 minutes. For a stove-top cooker, bring up to pressure over medium-high heat; reduce heat enough to maintain steady pressure. Cook 2 minutes. Remove from heat.

For both models, release pressure quickly. Carefully open lid. Sprinkle with pepper and serve with lemon wedges.

SLOW *4-HOUR LOW OR 2-HOUR HIGH COOK TIME*

Add ½ cup water to a 3½- or 4-qt. slow cooker. Arrange stuffed peppers, filling sides up, in cooker. Cover and cook on low 4 hours or high 2 hours. Sprinkle with pepper and serve with lemon wedges.

QUALITY CRABMEAT

Lump crabmeat is a combination of large chunks and small pieces of delicate white meat from the body of the crab. Look for it fresh; the best quality is refrigerated, not canned.

PER SERVING *413 cal., 27 g fat (12 g sat. fat), 120 mg chol., 1,087 mg sodium, 23 g carb., 3 g fiber, 9 g sugars, 20 g pro.*

NEW ENGLAND STYLE
CLAM CHOWDER

Makes 8 servings

- ½ lb. bacon, cut into ¼-inch pieces
- 3 medium potatoes, peeled and cut into ½-inch chunks (about 3 cups)
- 3 10-oz. cans whole baby clams with juice
- 1 cup chopped onion
- 2 cloves garlic, minced
- 2 bay leaves
- ½ tsp. salt
- ¼ tsp. black pepper
- 1 cup milk
- 2 cups half-and-half
- 3 Tbsp. all-purpose flour
- 2 Tbsp. butter, melted
- Oyster crackers (optional)
- Fresh thyme (optional)

FAST *5-MINUTE COOK TIME*

In a 6-qt. electric pressure cooker use the saute setting to cook bacon until crisp. For a stove-top cooker, cook directly in the pot over medium heat. Drain off fat. Reserve half the bacon to top chowder. Stir remaining bacon to scrape up any browned bits from bottom of pot. Add potatoes, juice from the clams (reserve clams), onion, garlic, bay leaves, salt, and pepper. Lock lid in place. Set an electric cooker on high pressure to cook 5 minutes. For a stove-top cooker, bring up to pressure over medium-high heat; reduce heat to maintain steady pressure. Cook 5 minutes. Remove from heat.

For both models, quickly release pressure. Carefully open lid. In a small bowl whisk together milk, half-and-half, flour, and butter. Gently stir milk mixture into pot. For an electric cooker, use the saute setting to bring to a simmer. Cook 5 minutes or until thickened and bubbly. Stir in the reserved clams. Simmer 1 minute more. For a stove-top cooker, cook directly in the pot. Remove and discard bay leaves. Top servings with reserved bacon, additional pepper, and, if desired, crackers and thyme.

SLOW *5-HOUR LOW OR 2½-HOUR HIGH COOK TIME + 30 MINUTES HIGH*

In a large skillet cook bacon until crisp; transfer to paper towels to drain. Reserve half the bacon to top chowder. In a 4- to 5-qt. slow cooker combine half the cooked bacon, the potatoes, juice from the clams (reserve clams), onion, garlic, bay leaves, salt, and pepper. Cover and cook on low 5 to 6 hours or high 2½ to 3 hours. Refrigerate reserved bacon and clams.

Meanwhile, in a small bowl whisk together milk, half-and-half, flour, and butter. Let stand at room temperature 30 minutes. If using low heat, turn to high. Gently stir milk mixture into cooker. Cover and cook 30 to 40 minutes more or until thickened and bubbly. Gently stir in reserved clams. Turn off cooker. Cover and let stand 10 minutes. Remove and discard bay leaves. Top servings with reserved bacon, additional pepper, and, if desired, crackers and thyme.

GO FRESH

If you are fortunate enough to find them, two pints of shucked fresh clams with liquid can be substituted for canned clams.

PER SERVING *312 cal., 15 g fat (7 g sat. fat), 116 mg chol., 898 mg sodium, 23 g carb., 1 g fiber, 5 g sugars, 25 g pro.*

SANDW
SAND
ES&WF
S&
WF

WICHE

RAPS

A cold meat sandwich is a cinch to make but not always satisfying. When you need a hot and hearty meal, take a spin through these dinner-worthy recipes.

BEER-SOAKED
BRISKET SANDWICHES

[WEEKNIGHT] --- [COMPANY]

Makes 10 servings

- 1 3½- to 4-lb. beef brisket (flat half), fat trimmed to ¼-inch thickness
- ½ tsp. salt
- ½ tsp. black pepper
- 1 Tbsp. vegetable oil
- 1 12-oz. bottle wheat beer
- 1 medium onion, sliced
- 4 cloves garlic, smashed and peeled
- ¼ cup Dijon-style mustard
- 1 Tbsp. hoisin sauce
- ¼ tsp. ground cloves
- 1 1-lb. loaf rectangular ciabatta bread, split, toasted, and cut into 3-inch pieces
- 2 medium carrots, peeled and cut into ribbons
  Napa cabbage
  Fresh Italian parsley (optional)

FAST _1½-HOUR COOK TIME_

Season brisket with salt and black pepper. In a 6-qt. electric pressure cooker, use the saute setting to cook meat, half at a time, in hot oil until browned. For a stove-top cooker, cook directly in the pot over medium-high heat. Remove beef; drain off fat. Add beer, onion, and garlic to pot. Stir to scrape up any browned bits from bottom of pot. In a bowl whisk together mustard, hoisin, and cloves. Spread over top of brisket. Place brisket in cooker on top of onion mixture. Lock lid in place. Set electric cooker on high pressure to cook 1½ hours. For stove-top cooker, bring up to pressure over medium-high heat; reduce heat enough to maintain steady pressure. Cook 1½ hours. Remove from heat.

For both models, quickly release pressure. Carefully open lid. Transfer meat to a platter; cover to keep warm. Skim fat from cooking liquid. Strain cooking liquid through a fine-mesh sieve lined with a double layer of 100%-cotton cheesecloth. Season with additional salt and pepper. Slice beef across the grain. Top bread with beef, carrots, and cabbage. If desired, top with parsley. Serve with cooking liquid.

SLOW _10-HOUR LOW OR 5-HOUR HIGH COOK TIME_

Season brisket with salt and black pepper. In an extra-large skillet cook meat, half at a time, in hot oil over medium-high heat until browned. In a 6-qt. slow cooker combine beer, onion, and garlic; top with brisket. In a bowl whisk together mustard, hoisin, and cloves. Spread over top of brisket. Cover and cook on low 10 to 12 hours or high 5 to 6 hours. Transfer meat to a platter; cover to keep warm. Skim fat from cooking liquid. Strain liquid through a fine-mesh sieve lined with a double layer of 100% cotton cheesecloth. Season to taste with additional salt and pepper. Slice beef across the grain. Top bread with beef, carrots, and cabbage. If desired, top with parsley. Serve with cooking liquid.

VEGGIE RIBBONS

To make ribbons from carrots (or parsnips, zucchini, or yellow squash), draw a vegetable peeler the length of the vegetable.

PER SERVING _427 cal., 17 g fat (6 g sat. fat), 106 mg chol., 559 mg sodium, 28 g carb., 2 g fiber, 3 g sugars, 37 g pro._

CUMIN-RED PEPPER FRENCH DIPS WITH APPLES

[WEEKNIGHT]---[HEALTHY]---[COMPANY]

Makes 12 servings

Nonstick cooking spray

1 2½-lb. boneless beef chuck roast, trimmed and cut into 2-inch pieces

3 cups halved and sliced red onions

3 Tbsp. packed brown sugar

1 Tbsp. Worcestershire sauce

1 tsp. ground cumin

¾ tsp. salt

½ tsp. crushed red pepper

½ cup 50%-less-sodium beef broth

12 ciabatta rolls, split

2 cups thinly sliced apples

FAST *45-MINUTE COOK TIME*

Lightly coat a 6-qt. electric or stove-top pressure cooker with cooking spray. Place meat in cooker. Top with the next six ingredients (through crushed red pepper); add broth. Lock lid in place. Set an electric cooker on high pressure to cook 45 minutes. For a stove-top cooker, bring up to pressure over medium-high heat; reduce heat enough to maintain steady pressure. Cook 45 minutes. Remove from heat.

For both models, let stand 15 minutes to release pressure naturally. Release any remaining pressure. Carefully open lid. Shred meat using two forks. Using a slotted spoon, divide roast and onions among rolls. Skim fat from cooking liquid and serve with sandwiches for dipping along with apple slices.

SLOW *11-HOUR LOW OR 5½-HOUR HIGH COOK TIME*

Lightly coat a 4-qt. slow cooker with cooking spray. Place meat in cooker. Add the next six ingredients (through crushed red pepper). Pour broth over mixture in cooker. Cover and cook on low 11 to 12 hours or high 5½ to 6 hours. Shred meat using two forks. Using a slotted spoon, divide roast and onions among rolls. Skim fat from cooking liquid and serve with sandwiches for dipping along with apple slices.

PER SERVING *337 cal., 11 g fat (5 g sat. fat), 65 mg chol., 509 mg sodium, 36 g carb., 3 g fiber, 8 g sugars, 23 g pro.*

CUBAN SHREDDED
BEEF SANDWICHES

Makes 6 servings

1 tsp. dried oregano, crushed

1 tsp. ground cumin

½ tsp. salt

½ tsp. black pepper

⅛ tsp. ground allspice

1 2- to 2½-lb. boneless beef chuck roast, trimmed and cut into 2-inch pieces

1 Tbsp. vegetable oil

2 medium onions, sliced

1 large green sweet pepper, halved, seeded, and sliced

4 cloves garlic, minced

¼ cup orange juice

¼ cup lime juice

6 bolillo or hoagie rolls, split and toasted

1 avocado, halved, seeded, peeled, and sliced

1 recipe Citrus Mayo

DIRECTIONS

In a bowl combine the first five ingredients (through allspice). Rub spice mixture onto all sides of the beef pieces. Prepare as directed for desired cooker, below.

FAST *30-MINUTE COOK TIME*

In a 4- to 6-qt. electric pressure cooker, use the saute setting to cook meat, half at a time, in hot oil until browned on all sides. For stove-top cooker, cook meat directly in the pot over medium-high heat. Remove beef; drain off fat. Place onions, sweet pepper, and garlic in pot. Add orange juice and lime juice. Place meat on vegetables. Lock lid in place. Set an electric cooker on high pressure to cook 30 minutes. For a stove-top cooker, bring up to pressure over medium-high heat; reduce heat enough to maintain steady pressure. Cook 30 minutes. Remove from heat. For both models, let stand 15 minutes to release pressure naturally. Release any remaining pressure. Carefully open lid. Using a slotted spoon, remove meat from pot. Shred meat using two forks; place shredded meat in a large bowl. Strain cooking liquid, reserving vegetables. Add ¼ to ½ cup cooking liquid to meat to moisten. Stir in reserved vegetables. Discard any remaining cooking liquid. Divide meat among rolls. Top with avocado. Spread about 2 tsp. Citrus Mayo on cut sides of roll tops.

SLOW *8-HOUR LOW OR 4-HOUR HIGH COOK TIME*

In a large skillet cook meat, half at a time, in hot oil over medium-high heat until browned on all sides. In a 4- to 6-qt. slow cooker layer onions, sweet pepper, and garlic. Pour orange juice and lime juice over vegetables. Place meat on vegetables. Cover and cook on low 8 hours or high 4 hours. Using a slotted spoon, remove meat from cooker. Shred meat using two forks; place shredded meat in a large bowl. Strain cooking liquid, reserving vegetables. Add ¼ to ½ cup cooking liquid to meat to moisten. Stir in reserved vegetables. Discard any remaining cooking liquid. Divide meat among rolls. Top with avocado. Spread about 2 tsp. Citrus Mayo on cut sides of roll tops.

CITRUS MAYO

Remove ½ tsp. grated zest and 1 tsp. juice from 1 orange. Remove ¼ tsp. zest and ½ tsp. juice from 1 lime. In a bowl whisk together zests, juices, ¼ cup reduced-fat mayonnaise, ⅛ tsp. salt, and a pinch of black pepper.

PER SERVING 383 cal., 12 g fat (3 g sat. fat), 64 mg chol., 702 mg sodium, 40 g carb., 4 g fiber, 4 g sugars, 28 g pro.

LOADED ITALIAN
GRINDER SANDWICHES

Makes 8 servings

- 1½ lb. bulk sweet or hot Italian sausage
- 8 oz. lean ground turkey
- 2 cups sliced fresh cremini or button mushrooms
- 2 15-oz. cans fire-roasted diced tomatoes, drained
- 1 medium green or red sweet pepper, chopped
- 1 medium onion, chopped
- 1 6-oz. can no-salt-added tomato paste
- 4 cloves garlic, minced
- 2 Tbsp. snipped fresh oregano or 2 tsp. dried oregano, crushed
- 8 Italian hoagie rolls, split
- 1 8-oz. pkg. shredded Italian-blend cheeses (2 cups)

  Sliced banana pepper (optional)

FAST 15-MINUTE COOK TIME

In a 6-qt. electric pressure cooker use the saute setting to cook and stir sausage, turkey, and mushrooms until meat is no longer pink. For a stove-top cooker, cook directly in pot over medium heat. Drain off fat. Stir tomatoes, sweet pepper, onion, tomato paste, garlic, and dried oregano (if using) into meat mixture in cooker. Set electric cooker on high pressure to cook 15 minutes. For stove-top cooker, bring up to pressure over medium-high heat; reduce heat enough to maintain steady pressure. Cook 15 minutes. Remove from heat.

For both models, let stand 15 minutes to release pressure naturally. Release any remaining pressure. Carefully open lid. Stir in fresh oregano (if using). Preheat broiler. Line an extra-large baking sheet with foil. Place roll tops, cut sides up, on prepared pan. Broil 5 to 6 inches from heat 1 to 2 minutes or until tops are lightly toasted. Remove roll tops from pan; set aside. Repeat with roll bottoms. Spoon meat mixture onto roll bottoms. Top with cheese. Broil 2 to 3 minutes or until cheese is melted and just starting to brown. If desired, top with banana peppers; add roll tops.

SLOW 8-HOUR LOW OR 4-HOUR HIGH COOK TIME

In a large skillet cook and stir sausage, turkey, and mushrooms over medium heat until meat is no longer pink. Drain off fat. Transfer meat mixture to a 5- to 6-qt. slow cooker. Stir tomatoes, sweet pepper, onion, tomato paste, garlic, and dried oregano (if using) into meat mixture. Cover and cook on low 8 to 10 hours or high 4 to 5 hours. Stir in fresh oregano (if using).

Preheat broiler. Line an extra-large baking sheet with foil. Place roll tops, cut sides up, on prepared pan. Broil 5 to 6 inches from heat 1 to 2 minutes or until tops are lightly toasted. Remove roll tops from pan; set aside. Repeat with roll bottoms. Spoon meat mixture onto roll bottoms. Top with cheese. Broil 2 to 3 minutes or until cheese is melted and just starting to brown. If desired, top with banana peppers; add roll tops.

PER SERVING 508 cal., 18 g fat (7 g sat. fat), 67 mg chol., 1,337 mg sodium, 50 g carb., 5 g fiber, 9 g sugars, 37 g pro.

PULLED PORK GYROS
WITH DILLED RADISH TZATZIKI

[WEEKNIGHT] ---[COMPANY]---

Makes 8 servings

- 1 5.3-oz. container Greek yogurt
- 1 small cucumber, shredded (¼ cup)
- ½ cup shredded radishes
- 2 Tbsp. snipped fresh dill weed
- 1 clove garlic, minced
  Salt and black pepper
- 2½ tsp. dried oregano, crushed
- 1½ tsp. dried marjoram, crushed
- 1½ tsp. garlic powder
- 1½ tsp. grated lemon zest
- 1 tsp. salt
- 1 tsp. black pepper
- 2 to 3 lb. boneless pork shoulder, trimmed and cut into large chunks
- ½ cup red wine
- 1 Tbsp. lemon juice
  Pita bread
  Sliced red onion
  Crumbled feta cheese
  Lemon wedges

DIRECTIONS

For tzatziki, in a medium bowl combine yogurt, cucumber, radishes, dill, and garlic. Season with salt and pepper to taste. Cover and chill until ready to serve. For seasoning mix, in a small bowl combine the next six ingredients (through the 1 tsp. pepper). Reserve 1 Tbsp. seasoning. Rub pork with remaining seasoning. Prepare as directed for desired cooker, below.

FAST   *60-MINUTE COOK TIME*

Place pork in a 4- to 6-qt. electric or stove-top pressure cooker. Add wine. Lock lid in place. Set an electric cooker on high pressure to cook 60 minutes. For a stove-top cooker, bring up to pressure over medium-high heat; reduce heat enough to maintain steady pressure. Cook 60 minutes. Remove from heat.

For both models, let stand 15 minutes to release pressure naturally. Release any remaining pressure. Carefully open lid. Using a slotted spoon, remove meat from cooker. Coarsely shred meat using two forks. Moisten with some of the cooking liquid. Add lemon juice and reserved seasoning; toss to combine. Serve meat on pita bread with tzatziki, sliced red onion, feta, and lemon wedges.

SLOW   *10-HOUR LOW OR 5-HOUR HIGH COOK TIME*

Place pork in a 3½- or 4-qt. slow cooker. Add wine. Cover and cook on low 10 to 12 hours or high 5 to 6 hours. Using a slotted spoon, remove meat from cooker. Coarsely shred meat using two forks. Moisten with some of the cooking liquid. Add lemon juice and reserved seasoning; toss to combine Serve meat on pita bread with tzatziki, sliced red onion, feta, and lemon wedges.

PER SERVING *379 cal, 10 g fat (4 g sat. fat), 79 mg chol., 856 mg sodium, 38 g carb., 2 g fiber, 3 g sugars, 30 g pro.*

PULLED PORK SANDWICHES WITH RED GINGER BBQ SAUCE

[WEEKNIGHT]----[HEALTHY]----[COMPANY]---

Makes 10 servings

- 2 tsp. ground cumin
- 2 tsp. ground coriander
- ¼ tsp. black pepper
- ⅛ tsp. salt
- 1 3- to 3½-lb. boneless pork shoulder roast, trimmed and cut into three pieces
- 1 cup beef broth
- 1 Tbsp. olive oil
- 1 cup chopped red onion
- 3 Tbsp. minced garlic
- 2 Tbsp. grated fresh ginger
- ⅔ cup packed brown sugar
- 1¼ cups red wine vinegar
- ¼ cup reduced-sodium soy sauce
- ½ tsp. crushed red pepper
- 1 14.5-oz. can diced tomatoes, undrained
- 10 bakery-style whole grain buns, split and toasted

DIRECTIONS

For spice rub, in a small bowl stir together cumin, coriander, black pepper, and salt. Sprinkle spice mixture over meat; rub in with your fingers. Prepare as directed for desired cooker, below.

FAST 25-MINUTE COOK TIME

Place a steam rack in a 6-qt. electric or stove-top pressure cooker; add broth. Place meat on rack in pot. Lock lid in place. Set an electric cooker on high pressure to cook 25 minutes. For a stove-top cooker, bring up to pressure over medium-high heat; reduce heat enough to maintain steady pressure. Cook 25 minutes. Remove from heat. For both models, let stand 15 minutes to release pressure naturally. Release any remaining pressure. Carefully open lid. Meanwhile, for sauce, in a large saucepan heat oil over medium-high heat. Add onion; cook 8 to 10 minutes or until very tender, stirring occasionally. Reduce heat if onion starts to get dark. Add garlic and ginger; cook and stir 2 minutes. Stir in brown sugar until melted. Add vinegar, soy sauce, and crushed red pepper. Bring to boiling; reduce heat. Boil gently, uncovered, 20 to 25 minutes or until reduced by half (about 1⅔ cups), stirring occasionally. Stir in tomatoes. Return to boiling; reduce heat. Boil gently, uncovered, 15 minutes. Remove meat, reserving cooking juices. Shred meat using two forks. Stir meat into sauce; heat through. Skim fat from cooking juices. Stir some juices into meat to moisten. Serve on buns.

SLOW 10-HOUR LOW OR 5-HOUR HIGH COOK TIME

Place meat in a 4- to 5-qt. slow cooker. Add broth. Cover and cook on low 10 to 12 hours or high 5 to 6 hours or until very tender.

For sauce, in a large saucepan heat oil over medium-high heat. Add onion; cook 8 to 10 minutes or until very tender, stirring occasionally. Reduce heat if onion starts to get dark. Add garlic and ginger; cook and stir 2 minutes. Stir in brown sugar until melted. Add vinegar, soy sauce, and crushed red pepper. Bring to boiling; reduce heat. Boil gently, uncovered, 20 to 25 minutes or until reduced by half (about 1⅔ cups), stirring occasionally. Stir in tomatoes. Return to boiling; reduce heat. Boil gently, uncovered, 15 minutes. Remove meat, reserving cooking juices. Shred meat using two forks. Stir meat into sauce; heat through. Skim fat from cooking juices. Stir some juices into meat mixture to moisten. Serve on buns.

PER SERVING 322 cal., 8 g fat (2 g sat. fat), 55 mg chol., 666 mg sodium, 35 g carb., 3 g fiber, 20 g sugars, 25 g pro.

GARLIC-GINGER PORK
LETTUCE WRAPS

Makes 10 servings

- ¼ cup reduced-sodium soy sauce
- 2 Tbsp. packed brown sugar
- 2 Tbsp. sherry or apple juice
- 1 Tbsp. minced garlic
- 2 tsp. grated fresh ginger
- 2 tsp. Asian chili garlic sauce
- 2 Tbsp. vegetable oil
- 2 to 2¼ lb. boneless pork loin chops, trimmed and cut into 1-inch cubes
- 1 cup chopped onion
- 1 8-oz. can water chestnuts, drained and finely chopped
- 1 large head butterhead (Boston or Bibb) lettuce, cored and separated into leaves

  Toppings, such as shredded carrots, sliced radishes, chopped peanuts, sliced green onions, and/or chopped fresh cilantro

DIRECTIONS

In a small bowl stir together soy sauce, brown sugar, sherry, garlic, ginger, and chili garlic sauce. Set aside. Prepare as directed for desired cooker, below.

FAST   6-MINUTE COOK TIME

In a 6-qt. electric pressure cooker use the saute setting to cook pork in hot oil 4 minutes or until lightly browned, in batches if necessary. for a stove-top cooker, cook directly in the pot over medium-high heat. Add onion and water chestnuts to pot. Pour soy sauce mixture over pork mixture. Lock lid in place. Set an electric cooker on high pressure to cook 6 minutes. For a stove-top cooker, bring up to pressure over medium-high heat; reduce heat enough to maintain steady pressure. Cook 6 minutes. Remove from heat.

For both models, quickly release pressure. Carefully open lid. Using a slotted spoon, divide pork among lettuce leaves. Add desired toppings.

SLOW   4-HOUR LOW OR 2-HOUR HIGH COOK TIME

In an extra-large skillet cook pork in hot oil over medium-high heat 4 minutes or until lightly browned, in batches if necessary. Transfer to a 3½- or 4-qt. slow cooker. Add onion and water chestnuts. Pour soy sauce mixture over pork mixture. Cover and cook on low 4 hours or high 2 hours or until pork is tender. Using a slotted spoon, divide pork among lettuce leaves. Add desired toppings.

HOT STUFF

Sambal oelek and sriracha are both chili garlic sauces that differ slightly. Sambal is a little chunkier and more vinegary, while sriracha is smoother and slightly sweeter.

PER SERVING *266 cal., 12 g fat (2 g sat. fat), 64 mg chol., 195 mg sodium, 11 g carb., 2 g fiber, 6 g sugars, 30 g pro.*

ASIAN-STYLE PULLED CHICKEN SLIDERS WITH SNOW PEA SLAW

Makes 6 servings

- ½ cup hoisin sauce
- 4 tsp. reduced-sodium soy sauce
- 4 tsp. minced fresh ginger
- 2 tsp. minced fresh garlic
- 2 tsp. packed brown sugar
- 2 tsp. rice vinegar
- 1 lime
- 3 Tbsp. mayonnaise
- 1 tsp. sugar
- 6 oz. snow pea pods, halved crosswise, then cut lengthwise into thin strips
- ½ cup shredded carrot
- 2 green onions, thinly sliced
- 2 lb. skinless, boneless chicken thighs
- 1 large sweet onion, halved lengthwise and thinly sliced (1½ cups)
- ½ cup chicken broth
- Slider buns

DIRECTIONS

For sauce, in a small bowl combine the first six ingredients (through rice vinegar); set aside. For Snow Pea Slaw, remove 1 tsp. grated zest and 1 Tbsp. juice from the lime. In a medium bowl combine the mayonnaise, lime juice and zest, and sugar. Add snow peas, carrot, and green onions; toss to coat. Cover and chill until ready to serve. Prepare as directed for desired cooker, below.

FAST *10-MINUTE COOK TIME*

In a 4- or 6-qt. electric or stove-top pressure cooker combine chicken and sweet onion. Drizzle with chicken broth and ⅓ cup of the sauce. Lock lid in place. Set an electric cooker on high pressure to cook 10 minutes. For a stove-top cooker, bring up to pressure over medium-high heat; reduce heat enough to maintain steady pressure. Cook 10 minutes. Remove from heat.

For both models, let stand 15 minutes to release pressure naturally. Release any remaining pressure. Using a slotted spoon, remove chicken and onion from cooker; discard cooking liquid. Shred chicken using two forks; transfer to a bowl or serving dish. Add the remaining sauce; toss to coat. Serve pulled chicken on buns with Snow Pea Slaw.

SLOW *6-HOUR LOW OR 3-HOUR HIGH COOK TIME*

In a 3½- or 4-qt. slow cooker combine chicken and sweet onion. Drizzle with chicken broth and ⅓ cup of the sauce. Cover and cook on low 6 hours or high 3 hours. Using a slotted spoon, remove chicken and onion from cooker; discard cooking liquid. Shred chicken using two forks; transfer to a bowl or serving dish. Add the remaining sauce; toss to coat. Serve pulled chicken on buns with Snow Pea Slaw.

PER SERVING 503 cal., 16 g fat (3 g sat. fat), 148 mg chol., 1,003 mg sodium, 50 g carb., 4 g fiber, 15 g sugars, 38 g pro.

CHICKEN SALSA TORTAS

Makes 6 servings

- 2 lb. skinless, boneless chicken breast halves
- 1 16-oz. jar salsa
- 1 tsp. dried oregano, crushed
- ½ tsp. garlic powder
- 6 bolillo rolls or hoagie buns, split
  Crumbled queso fresco
  Chopped fresh cilantro
  Shredded lettuce

FAST *15-MINUTE COOK TIME*

Place chicken in a 4- or 6-qt. electric or stove-top pressure cooker. In a small bowl stir together salsa, oregano, and garlic powder. Pour over chicken. Lock lid in place. Set an electric cooker on high pressure to cook 15 minutes. For a stove-top cooker, bring up to pressure over medium-high heat; reduce heat enough to maintain steady pressure. Cook 15 minutes. Remove from heat.

For both models, release pressure quickly. Carefully open lid. Transfer chicken to a cutting board, reserving liquid in cooker. Shred chicken using two forks. Transfer to a bowl. Stir some cooking liquid into chicken to moisten. Divide chicken among rolls. Top with cheese, cilantro, and lettuce.

SLOW *5-HOUR LOW COOK TIME*

Place chicken in a 3½- or 4-qt. slow cooker. In a small bowl stir together salsa, oregano, and garlic powder. Pour over chicken. Cover and cook on low 5 to 5½ hours. Transfer chicken to a cutting board, reserving liquid in cooker. Shred chicken using two forks. Transfer to a bowl. Stir some cooking liquid into chicken to moisten. Divide chicken among rolls. Top with cheese, cilantro, and lettuce.

ROLL WITH IT

Bolillo rolls are the Mexican variation of French baguettes. The 6-inch oval rolls are baked in a stone oven for a crunchy crust and soft interior.

PER SERVING *425 cal., 8 g fat (2 g sat. fat), 117 mg chol., 1,058 mg sodium, 41 g carb., 4 g fiber, 5 g sugars, 45 g pro.*

CASHEW CHICKEN WRAPS WITH SWEET-TANGY SLAW

Makes 8 servings

- ¼ cup rice vinegar
- 2 tsp. honey
- ½ tsp. salt
- 3 cups coarsely shredded red cabbage
- ⅔ cup slivered red onion
- 2 Tbsp. finely chopped fresh ginger
- 2 Tbsp. soy sauce
- 2 Tbsp. toasted sesame oil
- 2 Tbsp. honey
- ½ tsp. crushed red pepper
- 2½ to 3 lb. bone-in chicken thighs, skinned
- 2 cups fresh baby spinach leaves
- 8 large flour tortillas, warmed
- 1 cup chopped roasted cashews
- ½ cup thinly sliced green onions (optional)
- ½ cup chopped fresh cilantro (optional)

DIRECTIONS

For Sweet-Tangy Slaw, in a large bowl whisk together vinegar, the 2 tsp. honey, and the salt. Add cabbage and onion; toss until well coated. Cover; chill 2 hours or until ready to assemble wraps, stirring once or twice. For ginger seasoning, in a small bowl whisk together the next five ingredients (through crushed red pepper); set aside. Prepare as directed for desired cooker, below.

FAST *12-MINUTE COOK TIME*

Trim fat from chicken; place chicken in a 4-qt. electric or stove-top pressure cooker. Pour ginger seasoning over chicken. Set an electric cooker on high pressure to cook 12 minutes. For a stove-top cooker, bring up to pressure over medium-high heat; reduce heat enough to maintain steady pressure. Cook 12 minutes. Remove from heat.

For both models, quickly release pressure. Carefully open lid. Transfer chicken to a cutting board, reserving cooking liquid in pot. Allow chicken to cool until easy to handle. Remove chicken from bones; discard bones. Coarsely shred chicken using two forks. Return chicken to cooker with cooking liquid; toss to coat. Divide spinach among warm tortillas. Using a slotted spoon, top tortillas with chicken and Sweet-Tangy Slaw. Sprinkle with cashews. If desired, top with green onions and cilantro. Fold in sides; roll up tortillas. Cut wraps in half.

SLOW *5-HOUR LOW OR 2½-HOUR HIGH COOK TIME*

Trim fat from chicken; place chicken in a 3½- or 4-qt. slow cooker. Pour ginger seasoning over chicken. Cover and cook on low 5 to 6 hours or high 2½ to 3 hours. Transfer chicken to a cutting board, reserving cooking liquid in cooker. Allow chicken to cool until easy to handle. Remove chicken from bones; discard bones. Coarsely shred chicken using two forks.

Return chicken to cooker with cooking liquid; toss to coat. Divide spinach among warm tortillas. Using a slotted spoon, top tortillas with chicken and Sweet-Tangy Slaw. Sprinkle with cashews. If desired, top with green onions and cilantro. Fold in sides; roll up tortillas. Cut wraps in half.

PER SERVING *509 cal., 21 g fat (5 g sat. fat), 100 mg chol., 1,057 mg sodium, 52 g carb., 5 g fiber, 9 g sugars, 31 g pro.*

SOUPS & NO BOWLS

STEWS
ODLE

When winter has you weary, a warming bowl of soup or stew is comfort by the spoonful. Let one of these simple simmers take the chill away.

SWEET AND SPICY BEEF STEW

Makes 10 servings

- 2 tsp. ground cumin
- 1 tsp. salt
- 1 tsp. garlic powder
- 2 Tbsp. coconut oil
- 1 lb. ground beef
- 1 lb. boneless beef chuck, trimmed and cut into 1-inch cubes
- 2 cups coarsely chopped sweet onions
- 2 yellow, orange, and/or red sweet peppers, coarsely chopped
- 1 10-oz. sweet potato, peeled and coarsely chopped
- 2 28-oz. cans crushed tomatoes
- 1 cup beef broth
- 2 to 3 canned chipotle peppers in adobo sauce, chopped
- ¼ cup chopped fresh cilantro

DIRECTIONS

For the spice mix, in a small bowl stir together cumin, salt, and garlic powder. Prepare as directed for desired cooker, below.

FAST   *12-MINUTE COOK TIME*

In a 6-qt. electric pressure cooker use the saute setting to cook ground beef and half the spice mixture in 1 Tbsp. hot coconut oil until browned. For a stove-top cooker, cook directly in the pot over medium-high heat. Transfer meat to a bowl. Add remaining 1 Tbsp. coconut oil to pot. Add beef chuck and remaining spice mix. Cook and stir until browned. Return browned ground beef to pot. Add the next six ingredients (through chipotle peppers). Lock lid in place. Set an electric cooker on high pressure to cook 12 minutes. For a stove-top cooker, bring up to pressure over medium-high heat; reduce heat enough to maintain steady pressure. Cook 12 minutes. Remove from heat.

For both models, let stand 15 minutes to release pressure naturally. Release any remaining pressure. Carefully open lid. Stir in 2 Tbsp. cilantro. Top servings with remaining cilantro.

SLOW   *9-HOUR LOW OR 4½-HOUR HIGH COOK TIME*

In an extra-large skillet cook ground beef and half the spice mixture in 1 Tbsp. hot coconut oil over medium-high heat until browned. Transfer to a 5- to 6-qt. slow cooker. Add remaining 1 Tbsp. coconut oil to pot. Add beef chuck and remaining spice mix. Cook and stir until browned. Transfer to cooker. Add the next six ingredients (through chipotle peppers). Cover and cook on low 9 to 11 hours or high 4½ to 5½ hours. Stir in 2 Tbsp. cilantro. Top servings with remaining cilantro.

UP the flavor

Top servings of this sweet, spicy, and smoky stew with a spoonful of sour cream

PER SERVING *262 cal., 10 g fat (5 g sat. fat), 59 mg chol., 720 mg sodium, 22 g carb., 5 g fiber, 10 g sugars, 23 g pro.*

HOISIN BEEF STEW

Makes 4 servings

- 1½ lb. boneless beef chuck roast, trimmed and cut into 1½-inch cubes
- 1½ cups baby carrots
- 1 large onion, cut into ¼-inch wedges
- 1 8-oz. can sliced water chestnuts, drained
- ¾ cup beef broth
- ½ cup hoisin sauce
- 1 jalapeño pepper, seeded and finely chopped (tip p. 42)
- 1 Tbsp. grated fresh ginger
- 4 cloves garlic, minced
- 1 cup fresh snow pea pods or sugar snap peas
- 1 bunch green onions, thinly sliced
- Hot cooked rice

FAST *15-MINUTE COOK TIME*

In a 4- to 6-qt. electric or stove-top pressure cooker stir together the first nine ingredients (through garlic). Lock lid in place. Set an electric cooker on high pressure to cook 15 minutes. For a stove-top cooker, bring up to pressure over medium-high heat; reduce heat enough to maintain steady pressure. Cook 15 minutes. Remove from heat.

For both models, let stand 15 minutes to release pressure naturally. Release any remaining pressure. Carefully open lid. Stir in snow peas and green onions. Replace lid and let stand 10 minutes. Serve over rice.

SLOW *8-HOUR LOW OR 4-HOUR HIGH COOK TIME*

In a 4- to 5-qt. slow cooker stir together the first nine ingredients (through garlic). Cover and cook on low 8 to 10 hours or high 4 to 5 hours. Stir in snow peas and green onions. Replace lid and let stand 10 minutes. Serve over rice.

VEGGIE PERFECTION

Snow peas or sugar snap peas have the best flavor and texture—crisp-tender and bright green—when they are barely cooked. A few minutes in the hot cooked stew is plenty!

PER SERVING *494 cal., 12 g fat (5 g sat. fat), 118 mg chol., 863 mg sodium, 53 g carb., 5 g fiber, 17 g sugars, 41 g pro.*

OLD-FASHIONED BEEF STEW

Makes 6 servings

- ¼ cup all-purpose flour
- ½ tsp. salt
- ¼ tsp. black pepper
- 2 lb. beef chuck or beef stew meat, trimmed and cut into 1-inch cubes
- 3 Tbsp. vegetable oil
- 2 medium onions, cut into thin wedges
- 1 cup thinly sliced celery
- 4 red potatoes, cut into 1-inch cubes
- 4 carrots, bias-sliced ¼ inch thick
- 3 cups vegetable juice (2 cups for slow cooker)
- 3 cups reduced-sodium beef broth
- 2 Tbsp. Worcestershire sauce
- 1 tsp. dried oregano or thyme, crushed

DIRECTIONS

In a large resealable plastic bag combine flour, salt, and pepper. Add cubed meat to bag; shake bag to coat evenly. Prepare as directed for desired cooker, below.

FAST *12-MINUTE COOK TIME*

In a 6-qt. electric pressure cooker use the saute setting to cook meat, half at a time, in half the oil until browned. For a stove-top cooker, cook directly in the pot over medium-high heat. Return browned meat to pressure cooker. Add onions, celery, potatoes, and carrots. Combine 3 cups vegetable juice, the broth, Worcestershire sauce, and oregano. Pour over meat and vegetables. Lock lid in place. Set an electric cooker on high pressure to cook 12 minutes. For a stove-top cooker, bring up to pressure over medium-high heat; reduce heat enough to maintain steady pressure. Cook 12 minutes. Remove from heat.

For both models, let stand 15 minutes to release pressure naturally. Release any remaining pressure. Carefully open lid. Season to taste with additional salt and pepper.

SLOW *10-HOUR LOW OR 5-HOUR HIGH COOK TIME*

In a large skillet cook meat, half at a time, in half the oil over medium-high heat until browned. Transfer meat to a 4- to 6-qt. slow cooker. Add onions, celery, potatoes, and carrots. Combine 2 cups vegetable juice, the broth, Worcestershire sauce, and oregano. Pour over meat and vegetables. Cover and cook on low 10 to 12 hours or high 5 to 6 hours or until meat and vegetables are tender. Season to taste with additional salt and pepper.

UP the flavor

Top with crumbled cooked bacon or stir in coarse-grain mustard—or both!

PER SERVING *413 cal, 13 g fat (3 g sat. fat), 98 mg chol., 831 mg sodium, 33 g carb., 5 g fiber, 10 g sugars, 39 g pro.*

COUNTRY **LAMB STEW**

Makes 6 servings

- ¼ cup all-purpose flour
- ½ tsp. salt
- ¼ tsp. black pepper
- 1½ lb. boneless lean lamb or beef stew meat, cut into 1-inch cubes
- 2 Tbsp. vegetable oil
- 12 oz. red and/or yellow tiny new potatoes, halved or quartered
- 2 cups baby carrots
- 1 cup frozen pearl onions
- 2 cups chicken broth
- 1½ tsp. Greek seasoning
- 1 cup frozen peas
  Hot cooked Israeli couscous (optional)
  Plain Greek yogurt (optional)
  Chopped fresh oregano or Italian parsley (optional)

DIRECTIONS

In a large resealable plastic bag combine flour, salt, and pepper. Add cubed meat to bag; shake to evenly coat. Prepare as directed for desired cooker, below.

FAST   *15-MINUTE COOK TIME*

In a 6-qt. electric pressure cooker use the saute setting to cook meat, half at a time, in half the oil until browned. For a stove-top cooker, cook directly in the pot over medium-high heat. Return browned meat to pressure cooker. Add the next five ingredients (through Greek seasoning). Lock lid in place. Set an electric cooker on high pressure to cook 15 minutes. For a stove-top cooker, bring up to pressure over medium-high heat; reduce heat enough to maintain steady pressure. Cook 15 minutes. Remove from heat.

For both models, let stand 15 minutes to release pressure naturally. Release any remaining pressure. Carefully open lid. Stir in frozen peas. Cover; let stand 5 minutes. If desired, serve stew over couscous, top with yogurt, and sprinkle with oregano or parsley.

SLOW   *8-HOUR LOW OR 4-HOUR HIGH COOK TIME*

In a large skillet cook meat, half at a time, in hot oil over medium-high heat until browned. Transfer meat to a 4- to 6-qt. slow cooker. Add the next five ingredients (through Greek seasoning). Cover and cook on low 8 to 10 hours or high 4 to 5 hours. Turn off cooker. Stir in frozen peas. Cover; let stand 5 minutes. If desired, serve stew over couscous, top with yogurt, and sprinkle with oregano or parsley.

CHOOSE YOUR COUSCOUS

Israeli couscous (or pearl couscous) is shaped like tiny balls and available in most well-stocked grocery stores. As a substitute, use another small pasta or rice.

PER SERVING *295 cal, 11 g fat (6 g sat. fat), 72 mg chol., 636 mg sodium, 22 g carb., 4 g fiber, 5 g sugars, 27 g pro.*

LAMB, BEAN, AND
SWEET POTATO CHILI

Makes 8 servings

- 1½ lb. boneless lamb shoulder, trimmed and cut into 1-inch cubes
- 1 lb. sweet potatoes, peeled and cut into 2-inch pieces
- 2 15-oz. cans reduced-sodium black beans, rinsed and drained
- 2 14.5-oz. cans diced tomatoes, undrained
- 1 14.5-oz. can 50%-less-sodium beef broth
- 2 poblano chile peppers, seeded (if desired), and chopped (tip p. 42)
- 1 cup chopped onion
- ½ cup chopped carrot
- ½ cup chopped celery
- 1 tsp. salt
- 1 tsp. dried oregano, crushed
- 1 tsp. ground cumin
- 1 tsp. chili powder
- ½ tsp. black pepper
- 1 to 2 Tbsp. bottled hot sauce
- Plain fat-free Greek yogurt (optional)

FAST *20-MINUTE COOK TIME*

In a 6-qt. electric or stove-top pressure cooker combine the first 14 ingredients (through black pepper). Lock lid in place. Set an electric cooker on high pressure to cook 20 minutes. For a stove-top cooker, bring up to pressure over medium-high heat; reduce heat enough to maintain steady pressure. Cook 20 minutes. Remove from heat.

For both models, release pressure quickly. Carefully open lid. Stir in hot sauce. If desired, top servings with yogurt.

SLOW *7-HOUR LOW OR 3½-HOUR HIGH COOK TIME*

In a 5- to 6-qt. slow cooker combine the first 14 ingredients (through black pepper). Cover and cook on low 7 to 8 hours or high 3½ to 4 hours. Stir in hot sauce. If desired, top servings with yogurt.

SWAP IT OUT

Substitute beef chuck roast, trimmed and cut into 1-inch cubes, for the boneless lamb shoulder.

PER SERVING *376 cal., 15 g fat (7 g sat. fat), 53 mg chol., 1,028 mg sodium, 39 g carb., 9 g fiber, 7 g sugars, 23 g pro.*

SOUTHWEST BBQ PORK AND SQUASH STEW

Makes 8 servings

- 1½ lb. pork tenderloin, cut into 1-inch cubes
- 2 Tbsp. vegetable oil
- 1 medium onion, cut into wedges
- 2½ cups reduced-sodium chicken broth
- ½ cup bottled barbecue sauce
- 1 2-lb. butternut squash, seeded, peeled and cut into 1-inch cubes (6 cups)
- 2 medium carrots, cut into ½-inch pieces
- 1 poblano chile pepper, seeded and cut into 1-inch pieces (tip p. 42)
- 1 14.5-oz. can diced tomatoes with mild green chiles, undrained
- 1 Tbsp. chili powder
  Corn bread or corn muffins (optional)

FAST 20-MINUTE COOK TIME

In a 6-qt. electric pressure cooker use the saute setting to cook meat, half at a time, in half the oil until browned. For a stove-top cooker, cook meat directly in pot over medium heat. Return browned meat to cooker. Stir in the next eight ingredients (through chili powder). Lock lid in place. Set an electric cooker on high pressure to cook 20 minutes. For a stove-top cooker, bring up to pressure over medium-high heat; reduce heat enough to maintain steady pressure. Cook 20 minutes. Remove from heat.

For both models, let stand 15 minutes to release pressure naturally. Release any remaining pressure. Carefully open lid. If desired, serve with corn bread.

SLOW 8-HOUR LOW OR 4-HOUR HIGH COOK TIME

In a large skillet cook meat, half at a time, in half the oil over medium heat until browned. Transfer meat to a 6-qt. slow cooker. Stir in the next eight ingredients (through chili powder). Cover and cook on low 8 to 10 hours or high 4 to 5 hours. If desired, serve with corn bread.

PER SERVING 241 cal., 6 g fat (1 g sat. fat), 55 mg chol., 576 mg sodium, 27 g carb., 4 g fiber, 12 g sugars, 22 g pro.

PORK STEW WITH GREMOLATA

Makes 4 servings

- 1½ lb. boneless pork shoulder roast, trimmed and cut into 1-inch pieces
- 1 Tbsp. olive oil
- 1 14.5-oz. can diced tomatoes, undrained
- 1 14.5-oz. can beef broth
- 1 large onion, cut into thin wedges
- 1 cup sliced carrots
- ½ cup sliced celery
- ½ cup dry white wine
- 2 cloves garlic, minced
- ½ tsp. dried thyme, crushed
- ¼ tsp. salt
- ⅛ tsp. black pepper
- 1 Tbsp. butter, softened (pressure cooker only)
- 1 Tbsp. all-purpose flour (pressure cooker only)
- 1 Tbsp. quick-cooking tapicoa, crushed (slow cooker only)
- 2 cups hot cooked orzo pasta or rice
- 1 recipe Gremolata

FAST *10-MINUTE COOK TIME*

In a 4- or 6-qt. electric pressure cooker use the saute setting to cook meat, half at a time, in hot oil until browned. For a stove-top cooker, cook meat directly in pot over medium-high heat. Drain off fat. Stir in the next 10 ingredients (through pepper). Lock lid in place. Set an electric cooker on high pressure to cook 10 minutes. For a stove-top cooker, bring up to pressure over medium-high heat; reduce heat enough to maintain steady pressure. Cook 10 minutes. Remove from heat.

For both models, let stand 15 minutes to release pressure naturally. Release any remaining pressure. Carefully open lid. In a small bowl combine butter and flour; whisk into stew. Cook over medium heat until slightly thickened and bubbly. Serve stew over orzo and top with Gremolata.

SLOW *7-HOUR LOW OR 3½-HOUR HIGH COOK TIME*

In a large skillet cook meat, half at a time, in half the oil over medium heat until browned. Drain off fat. Transfer meat to a 3½- or 4-qt. slow cooker. Stir in the next 10 ingredients (through pepper) and the crushed tapioca. Cover and cook on low 7 to 8 hours or high 3½ to 4 hours. Serve stew over orzo and top with Gremolata.

GREMOLATA
In a small bowl combine ¼ cup snipped fresh Italian parsley, 2 tsp. grated lemon zest, and 4 cloves garlic, minced.

PER SERVING *480 cal., 16 g fat (6 g sat. fat), 109 mg chol., 936 mg sodium, 38 g carb., 5 g fiber, 7 g sugars, 39 g pro.*

HAM AND MIXED-BEAN SOUP WITH KALE

[WEEKNIGHT]---[HEALTHY]---

Makes 6 servings

- 1 cup mixed dried beans, such as kidney, pinto, cannellini, navy, and/or Great Northern
- 1½ lb. cooked smoked pork hocks or meaty ham bones
- 1 Tbsp. olive oil (pressure cooker only)
  Water (5 cups pressure cooker; 3 cups slow cooker)
- 1 14.5-oz. can reduced-sodium chicken broth
- 1½ cups sliced celery
- 1½ cups sliced carrots
- 1½ cups sliced leeks
- 2 Tbsp. snipped fresh rosemary or 2½ tsp. dried rosemary, crushed
- 1 bay leaf
- ¼ tsp. black pepper
- 3 cups torn kale
  Salt

FAST 40-MINUTE COOK TIME

Rinse beans; drain. In a 6-qt. electric pressure cooker use the saute setting to cook pork hocks in hot oil until browned. For a stove-top cooker, cook pork hocks directly in the pot over medium-high heat. Add beans, 5 cups water, and the next seven ingredients (through pepper). Lock lid in place. Set an electric cooker on high pressure to cook 40 minutes. For a stove-top cooker, bring up to pressure over medium-high heat; reduce heat enough to maintain steady pressure. Cook 40 minutes. Remove from heat.

For both models, let stand 15 minutes to release pressure naturally. Release any remaining pressure. Carefully open lid. Remove pork hocks and cool slightly. Remove and discard bay leaf. If desired, mash beans slightly. When hocks are cool enough to handle, cut meat off bones and chop meat; discard bones. Stir meat and kale into soup. Set electric cooker on saute setting or place stove-top cooker over medium heat; cook just until kale is wilted. Season to taste with salt and additional pepper.

SLOW 11-HOUR LOW OR 5½-HOUR HIGH COOK TIME

Rinse beans; drain. In a large saucepan combine beans and enough water to cover beans by 2 inches. Bring to boiling; reduce heat. Simmer, uncovered, 10 minutes. Remove from heat. Cover and let stand 1 hour. Drain and rinse beans. In a 5- to 6-qt. slow cooker combine beans, 3 cups water, and the next seven ingredients (through pepper). Cover and cook on low 11 to 13 hours or high 5½ to 6½ hours. Turn off cooker.

Remove pork hocks and cool slightly. Remove and discard bay leaf. If desired, mash beans slightly. When hocks are cool enough to handle, cut meat off bones and chop meat; discard bones. Stir meat and kale into soup. Let stand, covered, 10 minutes or just until kale is wilted. Season to taste with salt and additional pepper.

PER SERVING 275 cal., 11 g fat (4 g sat. fat), 35 mg chol., 675 mg sodium, 29 g carb., 11 g fiber, 4 g sugars, 18 g pro.

CHICKEN AND SAUSAGE STEW

Makes 6 servings

- 8 oz. dried cannellini or Great Northern beans (1¼ cups)
- 1½ lb. skinless, boneless chicken thighs, cut into 1-inch pieces
- 1 Tbsp. olive oil
- 4 cups chicken broth
- 1 large onion, cut into thin wedges (2 cups)
- 2 cups sliced fennel (tip p. 213)
- ½ cup beer or water
- 4 cloves garlic, minced
- 1½ tsp. fennel seeds, crushed
- 8 oz. smoked sausage, cut into 1-inch pieces
- Salt and black pepper

DIRECTIONS

In a 4-qt. Dutch oven combine beans and 4 cups water. Bring to boiling; reduce heat. Simmer, uncovered, 10 minutes. Remove from heat. Cover and let stand 1 hour. Drain and rinse beans. Prepare as directed for desired cooker, below.

FAST   *35-MINUTE COOK TIME*

In a 6-qt. electric pressure cooker use the saute setting to cook chicken in hot oil until browned. For a stove-top cooker, cook directly in pot over medium heat. Drain off fat. Add soaked beans to the pot. Stir in the next six ingredients (through fennel seeds). Lock lid in place. Set an electric cooker on high pressure to cook 35 minutes. For a stove-top cooker, bring up to pressure over medium-high heat; reduce heat enough to maintain steady pressure. Cook 35 minutes. Remove from heat.

For both models, let stand 15 minutes to release pressure naturally. Release any remaining pressure. Carefully open lid. Add sausage; let stand 5 minutes or until heated through. Season to taste with salt and pepper.

SLOW   *6-HOUR LOW OR 3-HOUR HIGH COOK TIME*

In a large skillet cook chicken in hot oil over medium heat until browned. Drain off fat. Add chicken and soaked beans to a 6-qt. slow cooker. Stir in the next six ingredients (through fennel seeds). Cover and cook on low 6 to 7 hours or high 3 to 3½ hours or until beans are tender. Add sausage; let stand 5 minutes or until heated through. Season to taste with salt and pepper

PER SERVING *460 cal., 18 g fat (5 g sat. fat), 130 mg chol., 918 mg sodium, 35 g carb., 10 g fiber, 5 g sugars, 39 g pro.*

GARAM MASALA CHICKEN STEW WITH PEAS AND POTATOES

Makes 6 servings

Nonstick cooking spray

6 large skinless, boneless chicken thighs (about 1½ lb. total)

2 large red potatoes, cut into ½-inch chunks (2 cups)

1 medium onion, thinly sliced

1½ tsp. grated fresh ginger

2 cloves garlic, minced

½ tsp. salt

½ tsp. black pepper

1 14.5-oz. can reduced-sodium chicken broth

1 8-oz. can no-salt-added tomato sauce

1 cup frozen peas

½ cup plain fat-free yogurt

1 to 1½ tsp. garam masala

FAST *12-MINUTE COOK TIME*

Lightly coat a 4- to 6-qt. electric or stove-top pressure cooker with cooking spray. In an electric cooker use the saute setting to cook chicken, half at a time, until browned. For a stove-top cooker, cook chicken directly in the pot over medium-high heat. Drain off fat. Return browned chicken to the pot. Add potatoes, onion, ginger, garlic, salt, and pepper. Pour broth and tomato sauce over mixture in pot. Lock lid in place. Set an electric cooker on high pressure to cook 12 minutes. For a stove-top cooker, bring up to pressure over medium-high heat; reduce heat enough to maintain steady pressure. Cook 12 minutes. Remove from heat.

For both models, let stand 15 minutes to release pressure naturally. Release any remaining pressure. Carefully open lid. Stir frozen peas, yogurt, and garam masala into stew. For an electric cooker, use the saute setting to simmer stew, uncovered, 5 minutes. For a stove-top cooker, simmer directly in the pot.

SLOW *5½-HOUR LOW OR 2¾-HOUR HIGH COOK TIME • 15 MINUTES HIGH*

Lightly coat a large skillet with cooking spray; heat skillet over medium-high heat. Add chicken; cook 6 minutes or until browned on both sides. In a 3½- or 4-qt. slow cooker combine potatoes, onion, ginger, and garlic. Top with chicken. Sprinkle with salt and pepper. Pour broth and tomato sauce over mixture in cooker. Cover and cook on low 5½ hours or high 2¾ hours. If using low, turn to high. Stir frozen peas, yogurt, and garam masala into stew. Cover and cook 15 minutes.

PER SERVING 231 cal., 5 g fat (1 g sat. fat), 107 mg chol., 643 mg sodium, 19 g carb., 4 g fiber, 6 g sugars, 27 g pro.

FRENCH CHICKEN STEW

Makes 8 servings

- 4 cups sliced fresh button and/or stemmed shiitake mushrooms
- 1 14.5-oz. can diced tomatoes, undrained
- 1 cup thinly bias-sliced carrots
- 1 medium red potato, cut into 1-inch pieces
- ½ cup chopped onion
- ½ cup fresh green beans, trimmed and cut into 1-inch pieces
- ½ cup pitted ripe olives, halved
- 1 cup reduced-sodium chicken broth
- ½ cup dry white wine or reduced-sodium chicken broth
- 1 tsp. dried herbes de Provence or Italian seasoning, crushed
- ¾ tsp. dried thyme, crushed
- ¼ tsp. coarse ground black pepper
- 8 skinless, boneless chicken thighs (1¾ to 2 lb. total)
- ½ tsp. seasoned salt
- 1 14- to 16-oz. jar Alfredo pasta sauce

FAST *8-MINUTE COOK TIME*

In a 6-qt. electric or stove-top pressure cooker combine the first seven ingredients (through olives). Stir in the next five ingredients (through pepper). Top with chicken; sprinkle with seasoned salt. Lock lid in place. Set an electric cooker on high pressure to cook 8 minutes. For a stove-top cooker, bring up to pressure over medium-high heat; reduce heat enough to maintain steady pressure. Cook 8 minutes. Remove from heat.

For both models, let stand 15 minutes to release pressure naturally. Release any remaining pressure. Carefully open lid. Stir in Alfredo sauce.

SLOW *6-HOUR LOW OR 3-HOUR HIGH COOK TIME*

In a 5- to 6-qt. slow cooker combine the first seven ingredients (through olives). Stir in the next five ingredients (through pepper). Top with chicken; sprinkle with seasoned salt. Cover and cook on low 6 to 7 hours or high 3 to 4 hours. Stir in Alfredo sauce.

PER SERVING 278 cal., 13 g fat (5 g sat. fat), 126 mg chol., 784 mg sodium, 13 g carb., 3 g fiber, 4 g sugars, 24 g pro.

CREAMY CAULIFLOWER AND SWEET POTATO SOUP

Makes 8 servings

- 1½ lb. orange-flesh sweet potatoes, peeled and cut into 1-inch pieces (4 cups)
- 4 cups cauliflower florets
- 1 cup chopped onion
- ½ cup chopped carrot
- 2 cloves garlic, minced
- 6 cups vegetable broth or reduced-sodium chicken broth
- 2 tsp. ground coriander
- 1 tsp. ground cumin
- ½ tsp. salt
- ½ tsp. ground ginger
- ⅛ tsp. cayenne pepper
- 1 cup canned unsweetened full-fat coconut milk (tip p. 118)
- Chopped fresh cilantro (optional)

FAST *6-MINUTE COOK TIME*

In a 6-qt. electric or stove-top pressure cooker combine the first 11 ingredients (through cayenne pepper). Lock lid in place. Set an electric cooker on high pressure to cook 6 minutes. For a stove-top cooker, bring up to pressure over medium-high heat; reduce heat enough to maintain steady pressure. Cook 6 minutes. Remove from heat.

For both models, let stand 15 minutes to release pressure naturally. Release any remaining pressure. Carefully open lid. Using a handheld immersion blender, blend soup until smooth. (Or let soup cool slightly. Transfer soup in batches to a food processor or blender. Cover and process or blend until smooth.) Stir in coconut milk. If desired, top servings with cilantro.

SLOW *6-HOUR LOW OR 3-HOUR HIGH COOK TIME*

In a 5- to 6-qt. slow cooker combine the first 11 ingredients (through cayenne pepper). Cover and cook on low 6 to 8 hours or high 3 to 4 hours. Using a handheld immersion blender, blend soup until smooth. (Or let soup cool slightly. Transfer soup in batches to a food processor or blender. Cover and process or blend until smooth.) Stir in coconut milk. If desired, top servings with cilantro.

GOOD TO KNOW

With an easy-to-use immersion blender, there's no need to transfer hot soup to a freestanding blender. Just submerge the blade end into the soup and puree away.

PER SERVING *161 cal., 5 g fat (5 g sat. fat), 0 mg chol., 829 mg sodium, 25 g carb., 4 g fiber, 7 g sugars, 3 g pro.*

INDIAN CHICKPEA AND VEGETABLE CURRY

[VEGETARIAN]---[COMPANY]---

Makes 4 servings

- 4 cups water
- 1 cup dried garbanzo beans (chickpeas)
- 1½ tsp. salt
- 4 medium carrots, cut into 1-inch pieces
- 2 medium onions, cut into ½-inch wedges
- ½ of a 28-oz. can crushed tomatoes (1½ cups)
- 4 cloves garlic, minced
- 1 serrano chile pepper, seeded (if desired) and finely chopped (tip p. 42)
- 1½ tsp. ground cumin
- 1½ tsp. ground coriander
- 1 tsp. ground ginger
- ¼ tsp. black pepper
- 1 cup frozen peas, thawed
- ⅓ cup chopped fresh cilantro
- ¼ cup heavy cream
  Hot cooked basmati rice (optional)
  Naan, warmed

FAST 50-MINUTE COOK TIME

In a 6-qt. electric or stove-top pressure cooker combine the water, beans, and ½ tsp. of the salt. Lock lid in place. Set an electric cooker on high pressure to cook 30 minutes. For a stove-top cooker, bring up to pressure over medium-high heat; reduce heat enough to maintain steady pressure. Cook 30 minutes. Remove from heat.

For both models, release pressure quickly. Carefully open lid. Drain beans, reserving ½ cup cooking liquid. Return beans to cooker. Add carrots, onions, remaining 1 tsp. salt, and reserved cooking liquid. Stir in tomatoes and next six ingredients (through black pepper). Lock lid in place. Set an electric cooker on high pressure to cook 20 minutes. For a stove-top cooker, bring up to pressure over medium-high heat; reduce heat enough to maintain steady pressure. Cook 20 minutes. Remove from heat.

For both models, release pressure quickly. Carefully open lid. Stir in peas, cilantro, and cream. Serve with rice (if desired) and naan for dipping.

SLOW 5½-HOUR HIGH COOK TIME

In a 4-qt. slow cooker combine the water, carrots, onions, beans, and ½ tsp. of the salt. Cover and cook on high 5 to 6 hours or just until beans are tender. Drain vegetables, reserving ½ cup of the cooking liquid. Return beans and vegetables to cooker. Stir in tomatoes and next six ingredients (through black pepper), remaining 1 tsp. salt, and reserved cooking liquid. Cover and cook 30 minutes. Stir in peas, cilantro, and cream. Serve with rice (if desired) and naan for dipping.

PER SERVING *470 cal., 11 g fat (4 g sat. fat), 17 mg chol., 1,375 mg sodium, 77 g carb., 13 g fiber, 19 g sugars, 19 g pro.*

PASTA, G
& LEG

GRAINS
LEGUMES

These recipes starring wholesome grains, earthy lentils, and savory pastas make it easier to eat less meat—and no one will complain. Not even the pickiest of eaters.

INDIAN-SPICED LENTILS
WITH SPINACH

Makes 6 servings

- 5 cups reduced-sodium chicken or vegetable broth
- 3 cups uncooked brown lentils, rinsed and drained
- 1 14.5-oz. can diced tomatoes, undrained
- 1 cup finely chopped carrots
- ½ cup chopped onion
- 2 serrano chile peppers, seeded and finely chopped (tip p. 42)
- 1 tsp. salt
- 1 tsp. ground cumin
- 1 tsp. ground coriander
- ½ tsp. ground turmeric
- 1 14-oz. can unsweetened coconut milk (tip p. 118)
- 1 5-oz. pkg. fresh baby spinach
  Black pepper
  Hot cooked basmati or brown rice
  Orange wedges

FAST 15-MINUTE COOK TIME

In a 6-qt. electric or stove-top pressure cooker combine the first 10 ingredients (through turmeric). Lock lid in place. Set an electric cooker on high pressure to cook 15 minutes. For a stove-top cooker, bring up to pressure over medium-high-heat; reduce heat enough to maintain steady pressure. Cook 15 minutes. Remove from heat.

For both models, let stand 15 minutes to release pressure naturally. Release remaining pressure. Carefully open lid. Stir in coconut milk and spinach. Season to taste with black pepper and additional salt. Serve over rice with orange wedges.

SLOW 8-HOUR LOW OR 4-HOUR HIGH COOK TIME

In a 5- to 6-qt. slow cooker combine the first 10 ingredients (through turmeric). Cover and cook on low 8 hours or high 4 hours. Stir in coconut milk and spinach. Season to taste with black pepper and additional salt. Serve over rice with orange wedges.

PER SERVING 484 cal., 9 g fat (8 g sat. fat), 0 mg chol., 823 mg sodium, 78 g carb., 10 g fiber, 5 g sugars, 23 g pro.

CHILI MAC AND CHEESE

Makes 9 servings

- 1 lb. ground beef
- 1 16-oz. pkg. dried penne pasta
- 2 Tbsp. all-purpose flour
- 1 Tbsp. chili powder
- ½ tsp. salt
- 4 cups water
- 1 15-oz. jar salsa con queso
- 1 2.25-oz. can sliced pitted ripe olives, drained
- 1 cup shredded Mexican-style cheese blend (4 oz.)
- Shredded lettuce
- Chopped tomatoes

FAST *5-MINUTE COOK TIME*

In a 6-qt. electric pressure cooker use the saute setting to cook ground beef until browned. For a stove-top cooker, cook directly in the pot over medium heat. Drain off fat. Stir in pasta, flour, chili powder, and salt. Stir in the water. Lock lid in place. Set an electric cooker on high pressure to cook 5 minutes. For a stove-top cooker, bring up to pressure over medium-high heat; reduce heat enough to maintain steady pressure. Cook 5 minutes. Remove from heat.

For both models, let stand 15 minutes to release pressure naturally. Release any remaining pressure. Carefully open lid. Stir in salsa con queso and olives. Top with cheese (do not stir). Cover; let stand 10 minutes. Stir gently to combine. Top servings with lettuce and tomatoes.

SLOW *2-HOUR HIGH COOK TIME*

In a large skillet cook ground beef over medium-high heat until browned. Drain off fat. Transfer meat to a 5- to 6-qt. slow cooker. Stir in pasta, flour, chili powder, and salt. Stir in the water. Cover and cook on high 2 hours, stirring once halfway through cooking. Stir in salsa con queso and olives. Top with cheese (do not stir). Cover; cook 10 minutes more. Stir gently to combine. Top servings with lettuce and tomatoes.

PER 1 CUP 427 cal., 18 g fat (7 g sat. fat), 50 mg chol., 691 mg sodium, 48 g carb., 3 g fiber, 3 g sugars, 19 g pro.

MAC AND FOUR CHEESES

Makes 4 to 6 servings

2 cups dry elbow macaroni

Nonstick cooking spray (slow cooker only)

1 12-oz. can evaporated milk

1 cup water

¼ cup finely chopped onion

½ tsp. garlic powder

¼ tsp. black pepper

⅛ tsp. cayenne pepper

1 cup shredded cheddar cheese (4 oz.)

1 cup Gruyère or Swiss cheese, shredded (4 oz.)

1 cup smoked Gouda cheese, shredded (4 oz.)

¼ cup finely shredded Parmesan cheese (1 oz.)

1 Tbsp. butter

½ cup panko bread crumbs

1 Tbsp. snipped fresh Italian parsley

½ tsp. smoked paprika

FAST *3-MINUTE COOK TIME*

In a 6-qt. electric or stove-top pressure cooker stir together first 11 ingredients (through Parmesan cheese). Lock the lid in place. Set an electric cooker on high pressure to cook 3 minutes. For a stove-top cooker, bring up to pressure over medium-high heat. Cook 3 minutes. Remove from heat.

For both models, let stand 15 minutes to release pressure naturally. Release any remaining pressure. Carefully open lid. Stir. Meanwhile, for the crispy topping, in a large skillet melt butter over medium heat. Add panko; cook and stir 2 minutes or until golden brown. Remove from heat; stir in parsley and smoked paprika. Sprinkle topping over macaroni.

SLOW *2½-HOUR LOW COOK TIME*

In a 4- to 5-qt. pot cook pasta in a large amount of boiling water 2 minutes. Drain. Rinse with cold water and drain again. Coat a 3½- or 4-qt. slow cooker with cooking spray. Add cooked pasta and next six ingredients (through cayenne pepper). Cover and cook on low 2 hours, turning the crockery liner a half turn after 1 hour of cooking, if possible.

Add cheeses. Stir to combine. Cover and cook 30 minutes more. Meanwhile, for the crispy topping, in a large skillet melt butter over medium heat. Add panko; cook and stir 2 minutes or until golden brown. Remove from heat; stir in parsley and smoked paprika. Sprinkle topping over macaroni.

PER 1⅓ CUPS SERVING *737 cal., 38 g fat (22 g sat. fat), 127 mg chol., 846 mg sodium, 59 g carb., 2 g fiber, 12 g sugars, 38 g pro.*

CHICKEN-ITALIAN SAUSAGE ZITI WITH SWEET PEPPERS

Makes 6 servings

- 12 oz. fully cooked Italian-style chicken sausage, halved lengthwise and sliced
- 2 red and/or yellow sweet peppers, coarsely chopped
- 1 28-oz. can diced tomatoes, undrained
- 1 8-oz. can tomato sauce
- ½ cup chicken broth
- 4 cloves garlic, minced
- 2 tsp. Italian seasoning, crushed
- 8 oz. dried ziti or bow tie pasta
- ½ cup chopped fresh basil
- 1 cup shredded provolone or mozzarella cheese (4 oz.)

FAST *8-MINUTE COOK TIME*

In a 6-qt. electric or stove-top pressure cooker combine the first seven ingredients (through Italian seasoning). For an electric cooker, bring to boiling using saute setting. For a stove-top cooker, cook directly in the pot over medium-high heat. Simmer, uncovered, 5 minutes. Stir in pasta. Lock lid in place. Set an electric cooker on high pressure to cook 8 minutes. For a stove-top cooker, bring up to pressure over medium-high heat; reduce heat enough to maintain steady pressure. Cook 8 minutes. Remove from heat.

For both models, let stand 15 minutes to release pressure naturally. Release any remaining pressure. Gently stir in basil. Top with cheese. Cover and let stand 5 minutes or until cheese is melted.

SLOW *6-HOUR LOW OR 3-HOUR HIGH COOK TIME+ 25 MINUTES HIGH*

In a 5- to 6-qt. slow cooker combine the first seven ingredients (through Italian seasoning). Cover and cook on low 6 to 7 hours or high 3 to 3½ hours. If using low, turn to high. Stir in pasta. Cover and cook 25 to 30 minutes more or just until pasta is tender, stirring after 10 minutes. Gently stir in basil. Top with cheese. Cover and let stand 5 minutes or until cheese is melted.

PER SERVING 350 cal., 11 g fat (5 g sat. fat), 57 mg chol., 1,080 mg sodium, 42 g carb., 5 g fiber, 8 g sugars, 22 g pro.

PASTA WITH BEEF-FENNEL RAGU

Makes 8 servings

- 1 lb. 93% lean ground beef
- 2 14.5-oz. cans diced tomatoes with basil, garlic, and oregano, undrained
- 2 cups thinly sliced fennel (tip p. 213)
- 2 cups reduced-sodium chicken broth
- 1 15-oz. can tomato sauce
- ⅓ cup chopped onion
- 4 cloves garlic, minced
- 1½ tsp. fennel seeds, lightly crushed
- 1 tsp. dried oregano, crushed
- ½ tsp. black pepper
- ¼ tsp. salt
- 1 12-oz. pkg. no-boil, no-drain penne pasta, such as Barilla Pronto
- ½ cup snipped fresh basil (tip p. 16)

FAST *2-MINUTE COOK TIME*

Break ground beef into bite-size pieces and place in a 6-qt. electric or stove-top pressure cooker. Add the next 11 ingredients (through pasta). Stir to combine. Lock lid in place. Set an electric cooker on high pressure to cook 2 minutes. For a stove-top cooker, bring up to pressure over medium-high heat; reduce heat enough to maintain steady pressure. Cook 2 minutes. Remove from heat.

For both models, let stand 5 minutes to release pressure naturally. Release any remaining pressure. Carefully open lid. If desired, let stand, covered, up to 10 minutes for pasta to reach desired doneness. Stir in basil.

SLOW *7-HOUR LOW OR 3½-HOUR HIGH COOK TIME + 20 MINUTES HIGH*

Break ground beef into bite-size pieces and place in a 6-qt. slow cooker. Add the next 10 ingredients (through salt). Stir to combine. Cover and cook on low 7 to 9 hours or high 3½ to 4½ hours. If using low, turn to high. Stir in pasta. Cover and cook 20 minutes more or just until pasta is tender, stirring after 10 minutes. Stir in basil.

PER SERVING *304 cal., 5 g fat (2 g sat. fat), 36 mg chol., 807 mg sodium, 46 g carb., 4 g fiber, 9 g sugars, 20 g pro.*

GRUYÈRE RISOTTO WITH ARUGULA GREMOLATA

Makes 4 servings

- ⅔ cup sliced leeks
- 2 cloves garlic, minced
- 1 Tbsp. butter
- 1¾ cups uncooked Arborio rice
- 4 cups reduced-sodium chicken broth
- ⅔ cup dry white wine
- ½ tsp. cracked black pepper
- 2 oz. Gruyère or Swiss cheese, shredded (½ cup)
- 1 recipe Arugula Gremolata

FAST *6-MINUTE COOK TIME*

In a 4- or 6-qt. electric pressure cooker use the saute setting to cook leeks and garlic in hot butter until tender. Stir in rice; cook and stir 1 minute more. Stir in broth, wine, and pepper. For a stove-top cooker, cook directly in the pot over medium heat. Lock lid in place. Set an electric cooker on high pressure to cook 6 minutes. For a stove-top cooker, bring up to pressure over medium-high heat; reduce heat enough to maintain steady pressure. Cook 6 minutes. Remove from heat.

For both models, release pressure quickly. Carefully open lid. Top with cheese and Arugula Gremolata.

SLOW *1¼-HOUR COOK TIME*

In a large skillet cook leeks and garlic in hot butter over medium heat 3 to 5 minutes or until tender. Stir in rice; cook and stir 1 minute more. Spoon rice mixture into a 3½- or 4-qt. slow cooker. Stir in broth, wine, and pepper. Cover and cook on high 1¼ hours or until rice is tender. Remove crockery liner from cooker, if possible, or turn off cooker. Let risotto stand, uncovered, 15 minutes before serving. Top with cheese and Arugula Gremolata.

ARUGULA GREMOLATA

In a small bowl stir together 1 cup snipped fresh arugula; 1 oz. prosciutto, crisp-cooked, drained, and crumbled; 2 Tbsp. chopped toasted pine nuts; 1 Tbsp. grated lemon zest; and 1 clove garlic, minced.

THE RIGHT RICE

Arborio rice has shorter, fatter kernels than long grain rice, with high starch content that makes this dish deliciously creamy.

PER SERVING *510 cal., 13 g fat (5 g sat. fat), 26 mg chol., 828 mg sodium, 74 g carb., 3 g fiber, 2 g sugars, 20 g pro.*

FARRO AND SHRIMP
WITH PARMESAN AND FETA

COMPANY

Makes 4 servings

- 1 14.5-oz. can reduced-sodium chicken broth
- 1 cup pearled farro, rinsed
- 4 cloves garlic, minced
- ¼ tsp. salt
- ¼ tsp. black pepper
- 1 lb. medium fresh or frozen shrimp, peeled and deveined
- 1 Tbsp. seafood seasoning (Old Bay)
- ¼ cup grated Parmesan cheese (1 oz.)
- 1 Tbsp. butter
- 1 8-oz. bunch Swiss chard, stems removed, leaves chopped (8 cups)
- 1 Tbsp. fresh lemon juice
- ¼ cup crumbled feta cheese (1 oz.)

FAST *13-MINUTE COOK TIME*

In a 4- or 6-qt. electric or stove-top pressure cooker combine the first five ingredients (through pepper.) Lock lid in place. Set an electric cooker on high pressure to cook 12 minutes. For a stove-top cooker, bring up to pressure over medium-high heat; reduce heat enough to maintain steady pressure. Cook 12 minutes. Remove from heat.

For both models, release pressure quickly. Carefully open lid. In a medium bowl stir together shrimp and seafood seasoning. Add to cooker. Lock lid in place. Set an electric cooker on high pressure to cook 1 minute. For a stove-top cooker, bring up to pressure over medium high-heat. Remove from or turn off heat after reaching pressure.

For both models, release pressure quickly. Carefully open lid. Add Parmesan cheese, butter, and Swiss chard to the cooker. Stir until chard is wilted. Stir in lemon juice. Top servings with feta cheese.

SLOW *2-HOUR HIGH COOK TIME*

In a 3½- or 4-qt. slow cooker combine the first five ingredients (through pepper.) Cover and cook on high 1½ hours. Meanwhile, in a medium bowl stir together shrimp and seafood seasoning. Add to cooker. Cook 30 to 45 minutes more or until farro is tender and shrimp is opaque. Add Parmesan cheese, butter, and Swiss chard to the cooker. Stir until chard is wilted. Stir in lemon juice. Top servings with feta cheese.

PER SERVING *364 cal, 8 g fat (4 g sat. fat), 203 mg chol., 1,351 mg sodium, 41 g carb., 6 g fiber, 2 g sugars, 35 g pro.*

FARRO, BLACK BEAN, AND SPINACH BURRITOS WITH TOMATO-AVOCADO SALSA

Makes 8 servings

- 1 cup chopped onion
- 2 cloves garlic, minced
- ¾ tsp. salt
- 1 Tbsp. olive oil
- 1 cup pearled farro, rinsed and drained
- 1 15-oz. can black beans, rinsed
- ¾ cup chopped red sweet pepper
- 3 cups vegetable broth
- 1 Tbsp. ground coriander
- 1 tsp. ground cumin
- 1 cup baby spinach
- 2 cups chopped tomato
- 1 large ripe avocado, halved, seeded, peeled, and diced
- 2 green onions, sliced
- ¼ cup snipped fresh cilantro
- 2 tsp. grated lime zest
- 1 Tbsp. lime juice
- 8 10-inch flour tortillas, warmed
- 1 cup shredded Monterey Jack cheese (4 oz.)

FAST *10-MINUTE COOK TIME*

In a 4- or 6-qt. electric pressure cooker use the saute setting cook onion, garlic, and ¼ tsp. of the salt in hot oil until tender. For a stove-top pressure cooker, cook directly in the pot over medium heat. Add farro, beans, red pepper, broth, coriander, and cumin. Set an electric cooker on high pressure to cook 10 minutes. For stove-top cooker, bring up to pressure over medium-high heat; reduce heat enough to maintain steady pressure. Cook 10 minutes. Remove from heat.

For both models, let stand 15 minutes to release pressure naturally. Release any remaining pressure. Carefully open lid. Drain, if necessary. Stir spinach into farro mixture.

For the Tomato-Avocado Salsa, in a small bowl combine tomato, avocado, green onions, cilantro, lime zest and juice, and remaining ½ tsp. salt. Divide farro mixture among warmed tortillas. Top with cheese and salsa. Fold bottom edge of each tortilla up and over filling; fold in opposite sides just until they meet. Roll up from the bottom.

SLOW *2-HOUR HIGH COOK TIME*

In a large skillet cook onion, garlic, and ¼ tsp. of the salt in hot oil over medium heat until tender. Transfer to a 3½- or 4-qt. slow cooker. Add farro, beans, red pepper, broth, coriander, and cumin.

Cover and cook on high 2 hours or until farro is tender. Drain, if necessary. Stir spinach into farro mixture.

For the Tomato-Avocado Salsa, in a small bowl combine tomato, avocado, green onions, cilantro, lime zest and juice, and remaining ½ tsp. salt. Divide farro mixture among warmed tortillas. Top with cheese and salsa. Fold bottom edge of each tortilla up and over filling; fold in opposite sides just until they meet. Roll up from the bottom.

PER SERVING *469 cal., 15 g fat (5 g sat. fat), 13 mg chol., 1,257 mg sodium, 69 g carb., 10 g fiber, 5 g sugars, 17 g pro.*

RED BEANS AND RICE

[WEEKNIGHT]

Makes 6 servings

- 1½ cups dried red kidney beans
- 2 cups reduced-sodium chicken broth
- 1 13.5- to 14-oz. pkg. andouille or kielbasa smoked sausage, sliced ½ inch thick
- 1 cup chopped onion
- ¾ cup chopped green sweet pepper
- ½ cup chopped celery
- 3 cloves garlic, minced
- ½ tsp. salt
- ¼ tsp. dried thyme, crushed
- ¼ tsp. dried oregano, crushed
- ¼ tsp. cayenne pepper
- 1 bay leaf
  Hot cooked white rice
  Sliced green onions

DIRECTIONS

In a large saucepan soak beans, covered, in 4 cups cold water in a cool place overnight.* Drain and rinse. Prepare as directed for desired cooker, below.

FAST *30-MINUTE COOK TIME*

Transfer beans to a 4- or 6-qt. electric or stove-top pressure cooker. Add broth and the next 10 ingredients (through bay leaf). Lock lid in place. Set an electric cooker on high pressure to cook 30 minutes. For a stove-top cooker, bring up to pressure over medium-high heat; reduce heat enough to maintain steady pressure. Cook 30 minutes. Remove from heat.

For both models, release pressure quickly. Carefully open lid. Remove and discard bay leaf. Serve beans and sausage with rice; top with green onions.

SLOW *10-HOUR LOW OR 5-HOUR HIGH COOK TIME*

Transfer beans to a 3½- or 4-qt. slow cooker. Add broth and the next 10 ingredients (through bay leaf). Cover and cook on low 10 to 11 hours or high 5 to 5½ hours. Remove and discard bay leaf. Serve beans and sausage with rice; top with green onions.

*QUICK SOAK METHOD
In a large saucepan combine beans and 4 cups water. Bring to boiling; reduce heat. Simmer, uncovered, 10 minutes. Remove from heat. Cover and let stand 1 hour. Drain and rinse.

SAUSAGE SMARTS

Andouille and kielbasa are both fully cooked smoked sausages. Cajun andouille is traditional (and ideal) for this dish because it infuses pleasant heat—but kielbasa works, too.

PER SERVING *474 cal., 18 g fat (6 g sat. fat), 40 mg chol., 990 mg sodium, 56 g carb., 8 g fiber, 3 g sugars, 22 g pro.*

MEDITERRANEAN CHICKEN AND WHEAT BERRY SALAD

Makes 8 servings

- 3 cups reduced-sodium chicken broth
- 1 14.5-oz. can no-salt-added diced fire-roasted tomatoes, undrained
- 1½ cups uncooked wheat berries
- ¾ cup chopped cucumber
- ½ cup chopped fresh Italian parsley
- ¼ cup thinly sliced green onions
- 1 Tbsp. snipped fresh mint
- ¼ cup lemon juice
- 2 Tbsp. olive oil
- ½ tsp. ground cumin
- ¼ tsp. garlic salt
- 1 lb. chopped cooked chicken or shrimp
- ¼ cup crumbled feta cheese (1 oz.)

FAST *35-MINUTE COOK TIME*

In a 6-qt. electric or stove-top pressure cooker combine broth, tomatoes, and wheat berries. Lock lid in place. Set an electric cooker on high pressure to cook 35 minutes. For a stove-top cooker, bring up to pressure over medium-high heat; reduce heat enough to maintain steady pressure. Cook 35 minutes. Remove from heat.

For both models, let stand 15 minutes to release pressure naturally. Release any remaining pressure. Carefully open lid. Using a slotted spoon, transfer wheat berry mixture to a large bowl; discard liquid in cooker. Cool wheat berries to room temperature. Stir in the next four ingredients (through mint).

For dressing, in a screw-top jar combine the next four ingredients (through garlic salt). Cover and shake well. Pour dressing over wheat berry mixture; toss gently to coat. Stir in chicken. Cover and chill 4 to 24 hours. Sprinkle with cheese before serving.

SLOW *7½-HOUR LOW COOK TIME*

In a 4- to 5-qt. slow cooker combine broth, tomatoes, and wheat berries. Cover and cook on low 7½ to 8 hours or until wheat berries are tender. Using a slotted spoon, transfer wheat berry mixture to a large bowl; discard liquid in cooker. Cool wheat berries to room temperature. Stir in the next four ingredients (through mint).

For dressing, in a screw-top jar combine the next four ingredients (through garlic salt). Cover and shake well. Pour dressing over wheat berry mixture; toss gently to coat. Stir in chicken. Cover and chill 4 to 24 hours. Sprinkle with cheese before serving.

PER SERVING *294 cal., 9 g fat (2 g sat. fat), 55 mg chol., 339 mg sodium, 29 g carb., 5 g fiber, 2 g sugars, 24 g pro.*

SPANISH CHICKPEAS
AND TOMATOES OVER RICE

Makes 4 servings

- 8 oz. dried chickpeas
- 1 28-oz. can whole San Marzano tomatoes, cut up, undrained
- 1 14.5-oz. can reduced-sodium chicken broth
- ½ cup chopped red onion
- 3 cloves garlic, minced
- ½ tsp. smoked paprika
- ½ tsp. ground coriander
- ½ tsp. dried oregano, crushed
- ½ tsp. dried dill weed
- ¼ tsp. salt
- ¼ tsp. black pepper
- 2 Tbsp. lemon juice
- 1 5-oz. pkg. baby spinach
  Hot cooked brown rice
- ¼ cup chopped fresh Italian parsley
- 4 oz. goat cheese (chèvre)

DIRECTIONS
In a 4- to 5-qt. Dutch oven soak beans, covered, in 8 cups cold water in a cool place overnight.* Drain and rinse. Prepare as directed for desired cooker, below.

FAST *15-MINUTE COOK TIME*

In a 4- to 6-qt. electric or stove-top pressure cooker place drained chickpeas and the next 10 ingredients (through pepper). Lock lid in place. Set an electric cooker on high pressure to cook 15 minutes. For a stove-top cooker, bring up to pressure over medium-high heat; reduce heat enough to maintain steady pressure. Cook 15 minutes. Remove from heat.

For both models, let stand 15 minutes to release pressure naturally. Stir in lemon juice and spinach. Cover and let stand 3 minutes or until spinach is wilted. Serve over rice. Top with parsley and goat cheese.

SLOW *5½-HOUR HIGH COOK TIME*

In a 3½-qt. slow cooker place drained chickpeas and the next 10 ingredients (through pepper). Cover and cook on high 5½ to 6 hours or until beans are tender. Stir in lemon juice and spinach. Cover and let stand 3 minutes or until spinach is wilted. Serve over rice. Top with parsley and goat cheese.

*QUICK SOAK METHOD
In a 4- to 5-qt. Dutch oven combine beans and 8 cups water. Bring to boiling; reduce heat. Simmer, uncovered, 10 minutes. Remove from heat. Cover and let stand 1 hour. Drain and rinse.

MAKE IT VEGETARIAN

To make this dish vegetarian, swap out the chicken broth for vegetable broth. To make it vegan, skip the goat cheese and top with toasted slivered almonds instead.

PER SERVING *514 cal., 13 g fat (6 g sat. fat), 22 mg chol., 704 mg sodium, 75 g carb., 12 g fiber, 15 g sugars, 25 g pro.*

SMOKY **CASSOULET**

Makes 6 servings

2 cups dried navy beans

6 oz. cooked kielbasa, thinly sliced

3 oz. pancetta, chopped

1 cup chopped onion

⅔ cup coarsely chopped carrots

⅓ cup thinly sliced celery

3 cloves garlic, minced

1 tsp. dried thyme, crushed

1 bay leaf

4 cups reduced-sodium chicken broth

¼ cup dry white wine (optional)

Chopped fresh Italian parsley

DIRECTIONS

Rinse beans. In a large pot combine beans and 8 cups water. Bring to boiling; reduce heat. Simmer, uncovered, 2 minutes. Remove from heat. Cover and let stand 1 hour. Drain and rinse beans. Prepare as directed for desired cooker, below.

FAST *35-MINUTE COOK TIME*

In a 6-qt. electric or stove-top pressure cooker combine beans and the next eight ingredients (through bay leaf). Pour broth over all. Set an electric cooker on high pressure to cook 35 minutes. For a stove-top cooker, bring up to pressure over medium-high heat; reduce heat enough to maintain steady pressure. Cook 35 minutes. Remove from heat.

For both models, let stand to release pressure naturally. Carefully open lid. Remove and discard bay leaf. Stir in wine, if desired. Top servings with parsley.

SLOW *9-HOUR LOW OR 4½-HOUR HIGH COOK TIME*

In a 5- to 6-qt. slow cooker combine beans and the next eight ingredients (through bay leaf). Pour broth over all. Cover and cook on low 9 to 10 hours or high 4½ to 5 hours. Remove and discard bay leaf. Stir in wine, if desired. Top servings with parsley.

SPEEDY BEANS

While a slow cooker works fine for cooking beans, the pressure cooker certainly wins out in terms of time. You get creamy, tender beans in a fraction of the time it takes in a slow cooker.

PER SERVING *394 cal., 14 g fat (4 g sat. fat), 22 mg chol., 742 mg sodium, 47 g carb., 11 g fiber, 5 g sugars, 23 g pro.*

SMOKY APRICOT-BACON
BAKED BEANS

Makes 16 servings

- 1 lb. dry navy or Great Northern beans
- 6 slices bacon, crisp-cooked and crumbled
- ½ cup chopped dried apricots
- 1½ cups chopped onion
- 1 8-oz. can tomato sauce
- ½ cup packed brown sugar
- ½ cup apricot preserves
- 2 tsp. ground ancho chile pepper or chili powder
- 1 tsp. dry mustard
- 1 tsp. smoked paprika
- ½ tsp. salt
- ½ tsp. black pepper
- 2 Tbsp. apple cider vinegar
- Crumbled crisp-cooked bacon (optional)

DIRECTIONS

In a 4- to 5-qt. Dutch oven combine beans and 8 cups water. Bring to boiling; reduce heat. Simmer, uncovered, 10 minutes. Remove from heat. Cover and let stand 1 hour. Drain and rinse beans. Prepare as directed for desired cooker, below.

FAST *45-MINUTE COOK TIME*

In a 6-qt. electric or stove-top pressure cooker combine beans and the next 11 ingredients (through black pepper). Stir in 2½ cups fresh water. Lock lid in place. Set an electric cooker on high pressure to cook 45 minutes. For a stove-top cooker, bring up to pressure over medium-high heat; reduce heat enough to maintain steady pressure. Cook 45 minutes. Remove from heat.

For both models, let stand 15 minutes to release pressure naturally. Release any remaining pressure. Carefully open lid. Stir in vinegar. If desired, sprinkle with additional bacon.

SLOW *7½-HOUR HIGH COOK TIME*

In a 5- to 6-qt. slow cooker combine beans and the next 11 ingredients (through black pepper). Stir in 2½ cups fresh water. Cover and cook on high 7½ to 8 hours. Stir in vinegar. If desired, sprinkle with additional bacon.

PER SERVING 182 cal., 2 g fat (0 g sat. fat), 3 mg chol., 198 mg sodium, 35 g carb., 5 g fiber, 16 g sugars, 8 g pro.

SALA
& SID

ADS &
ES

While the main course bubbles away in the appliance of your choosing, whip up one of these refreshing salads, vegetable sides, or fresh-baked breads to serve alongside.

ROASTED ONIONS AND FENNEL
WITH PROSCIUTTO

Makes 6 servings

- 3 medium fennel bulbs,* trimmed and cut into 1-inch wedges
- 2 medium red onions, cut into 1-inch wedges
- 2 Tbsp. olive oil
- ¼ tsp. salt
- ¼ tsp. black pepper
- 2 oz. prosciutto, cut into shreds
- 2 Tbsp. finely shredded Asiago cheese
- 1 tsp. snipped fresh thyme
  Snipped fennel fronds

DIRECTIONS

Preheat oven to 400°F. In a shallow baking pan combine fennel and onion wedges. Drizzle with oil and sprinkle with salt and pepper; toss to coat.

Roast 35 to 40 minutes or until tender and lightly browned, stirring occasionally. Sprinkle with remaining ingredients.

*INGREDIENT KNOW-HOW

To trim a fennel bulb, cut off the stalk about 1 inch above the bulb. Cut the bulb in half straight through the root. Remove and discard any wilted outer layers of the bulb. Cut a thin slice of the fennel bulb off the root end and discard. Wash the fennel under cool water; pat dry with paper towels. Stand the bulb upright, then cut the bulb in half lengthwise. Cut each half into two pieces to make quarters. Cut away and discard the tough core from each quarter. Then slice or chop the fennel according to the recipe.

PER SERVING *132 cal., 8 g fat (1 g sat. fat), 3 mg chol., 353 mg sodium, 12 g carb., 4 g fiber, 2 g sugars, 5 g pro.*

ORANGE- AND BALSAMIC- GLAZED TRICOLOR CARROTS

Makes 6 servings

- 2 lb. medium red, yellow, and/or orange carrots, peeled
- ½ cup orange juice
- ¼ cup balsamic vinegar
- 4 tsp. sugar
- ¾ tsp. salt
- ¼ tsp. black pepper
- 2 Tbsp. butter
- 1 Tbsp. snipped fresh chives

DIRECTIONS

Place a steamer basket in a large saucepan. Add water to just below the bottom of the basket. Bring water to boiling. Add carrots to steamer basket. Cover; reduce heat. Steam 15 to 20 minutes or just until carrots are tender. Transfer carrots to a serving platter; cover to keep warm.

Meanwhile, for glaze, in a medium saucepan combine orange juice, vinegar, sugar, salt, and pepper. Bring to boiling; reduce heat. Simmer, uncovered, 12 minutes or until reduced to a syrupy consistency (about ⅓ cup). Stir in butter. Drizzle glaze over carrots and sprinkle with chives.

UP the flavor

Give this sweet side some zip with a little crushed red pepper in the glaze.

PER SERVING 126 cal., 4 g fat (2 g sat. fat), 10 mg chol., 432 mg sodium, 21 g carb., 4 g fiber, 13 g sugars, 2 g pro.

SPICE-AND-HONEY
ROASTED CARROTS

Makes 6 servings

- 1½ lb. regular or tricolor carrots
- 1 Tbsp. olive oil
- ½ cup coarsely chopped hazelnuts
- 1 Tbsp. coriander seeds
- 1 Tbsp. sesame seeds
- 1½ tsp. cumin seeds
- ½ tsp. salt
- ¼ tsp. black pepper
- 1 Tbsp. honey

DIRECTIONS

Preheat oven to 425°F. Trim carrots and peel if desired. Halve large carrots lengthwise. Line a 15×10-inch baking pan with parchment paper or foil. Spread carrots in the prepared pan. Drizzle with olive oil. Roast, uncovered, 20 minutes. Meanwhile, heat a skillet over medium-high heat. Add hazelnuts; cook 3 minutes or until fragrant and toasted, stirring occasionally. Transfer nuts to a bowl. Add seeds to hot skillet. Cook over medium-high heat 2 minutes or until fragrant and toasted, stirring constantly. Remove spices from heat and transfer to another bowl; cool 10 minutes.

Using a spice or coffee grinder or mortar and pestle, grind or crush toasted spices just until coarsely ground. Add the hazelnuts, salt, and pepper, crushing nuts slightly. Remove carrots from the oven. Drizzle with honey; toss to coat. Sprinkle carrots with half the hazelnut mixture. Roast 5 to 10 minutes or until carrots are tender. Transfer carrots to a serving platter. Sprinkle with more nut seasoning and, if desired, drizzle with additional honey.

PER SERVING *152 cal., 9 g fat (1 g sat. fat), 0 mg chol., 274 mg sodium, 17 g carb., 5 g fiber, 9 g sugars, 3 g pro.*

INDIAN-SCENTED ROASTED BEETS AND CARROTS WITH LIME-CILANTRO CREAM

Makes 10 servings

- 2½ lb. medium beets, trimmed, peeled, and cut into wedges (6 cups)
- 8 oz. slender carrots, bias-sliced into 2-inch pieces
- ¼ cup olive oil
- ¾ tsp. kosher salt
- ¼ tsp. black pepper
- 1 lime
- 1 Tbsp. honey
- 1 clove garlic, minced
- ½ tsp. ground coriander
- ½ tsp. ground cumin
- ¼ tsp. crushed red pepper
- 1 6-oz. carton plain Greek yogurt
- ¼ cup snipped fresh cilantro
- 1 tsp. grated fresh ginger

DIRECTIONS

Place beets in the center of a piece of heavy foil. Place carrots on another piece of foil. Drizzle vegetables with 2 Tbsp. of the oil and sprinkle with ¼ tsp. of the salt and the black pepper. Wrap tightly in foil and stack in a 6-qt. slow cooker. Cover and cook on high 4 to 5 hours or until tender. Meanwhile, remove ½ tsp. grated zest and 1 Tbsp. juice from the lime. For dressing, in a small bowl whisk together the lime juice, remaining 2 Tbsp. oil, remaining ½ tsp. salt, the honey, garlic, coriander, cumin, and crushed red pepper.

Remove foil packets from cooker. Open packets, reserving liquid. Place beets, carrots, and liquid from packets in the cooker. Drizzle with the dressing; toss to coat. For lime-cilantro cream, in a small bowl combine yogurt, lime zest, cilantro, and ginger. Serve vegetables with the cream, and, if desired, sprinkle with additional crushed red pepper.

WE'VE GOT THE BEETS!

Beautiful red beets bleed when cut and the juice can stain. As an option, substitute yellow or golden beets. While the color is different, taste and texture remain the same.

PER SERVING *127 cal., 6 g fat (1 g sat. fat), 1 mg chol., 258 mg sodium, 16 g carb., 4 g fiber, 11 g sugars, 4 g pro.*

ROASTED CABBAGE **WITH PEARS**

[VEGETARIAN]---[COMPANY]---

Makes 4 servings

1   1½-lb. head savoy, green, or red cabbage, trimmed and cut into 8 wedges

Olive oil

Salt

Black pepper

3   pears, halved lengthwise and cored

2   Tbsp. fresh lemon juice

¾   cup chopped walnuts, toasted (tip p. 20)

½   cup crumbled blue cheese

DIRECTIONS

Preheat oven to 425°F. Place cabbage in a 15×10-inch baking pan. Drizzle with oil and sprinkle with salt and pepper.

Roast 35 to 40 minutes or until tender, turning cabbage once and adding pears the last 10 to 15 minutes. Drizzle lemon juice over cabbage and pears. Sprinkle with walnuts and cheese.

PICK PEARS

When cooking pears, choose a variety that holds up to heat, such as Bosc or Anjou, to retain shape and texture. Bartletts will do in a pinch; avoid Comice, which fall apart when cooked.

PER SERVING *364 cal., 25 g fat (5 g sat. fat), 11 mg chol., 529 mg sodium, 32 g carb., 10 g fiber, 16 g sugars, 10 g pro.*

QUICK SAUERKRAUT AND APPLES

[VEGETARIAN]

Makes 8 servings

- 2 Tbsp. unsalted butter
- 1 cup thinly sliced onion
- 4 lb. refrigerated sauerkraut, rinsed and drained
- 2 cups thinly sliced Gala, Fuji, or Red Delicious apples
- 1 cup dry white wine
- 3 to 4 Tbsp. packed dark brown sugar
- ½ tsp. kosher salt
- ½ tsp. black pepper
- 1 cup chopped Gala, Fuji, or Red Delicious apple (optional)
- 1 to 2 Tbsp. unsalted butter (optional)
- 1 Tbsp. snipped fresh dill (optional)

DIRECTIONS

In a 4- to 5-qt. heavy Dutch oven melt 2 Tbsp. butter over medium-high heat. Add onion; cook 6 minutes or until golden, stirring occasionally. Stir in sauerkraut, sliced apples, and wine. Bring to boiling; reduce heat. Simmer, covered, 1 hour or until sauerkraut is tender, stirring occasionally. Stir in brown sugar, salt, and pepper.

If desired, in a medium skillet cook chopped apple in 1 to 2 Tbsp. butter just until softened. Top sauerkraut with chopped apple and, if desired, dill.

PER SERVING 141 cal., 3 g fat (2 g sat. fat), 8 mg chol., 773 mg sodium, 21 g carb., 7 g fiber, 13 g sugars, 2 g pro.

INDIAN-SPICED ROASTED PEAS

Makes 5 servings

2	Tbsp. coconut oil
½	tsp. curry powder
¼	tsp. salt
¼	tsp. black pepper
16	oz. fresh sugar snap pea pods (5 cups) or snow pea pods (12 oz.), strings removed
¼	cup plain Greek yogurt
1	Tbsp. snipped fresh mint
	Dash salt
	Lemon wedges

DIRECTIONS

Preheat oven to 450°F. In a small bowl microwave oil 10 seconds or until melted. Stir in curry powder, salt, and pepper. Place pea pods in a 15×10-inch baking pan. Drizzle with oil mixture; toss to coat.

Roast 15 minutes or until tender and brown, stirring once. Transfer to a serving dish. In a small bowl combine yogurt, mint, and a dash of salt. Serve peas with minted yogurt and lemon wedges.

PER SERVING 101 cal., 6 g fat (5 g sat. fat), 1 mg chol., 163 mg sodium, 10 g carb., 4 g fiber, 5 g sugars, 4 g pro.

PARMESAN-ROASTED
CAULIFLOWER

Makes 8 servings

- 6 cups cauliflower florets
- 1 Tbsp. olive oil
- Salt and black pepper
- ½ cup shredded Parmesan cheese (2 oz.)
- ¼ cup butter
- 2 cloves garlic, minced
- ⅔ cup slivered almonds, chopped
- ⅔ cup panko bread crumbs

DIRECTIONS

Preheat oven to 450°F. Place cauliflower in a 15×10-inch baking pan. Drizzle with oil and sprinkle with salt and pepper; toss to coat. Roast 20 minutes. Stir in cheese. Roast 3 to 5 minutes more or until cauliflower is crisp-tender.

Meanwhile, in a medium skillet melt butter over medium heat. Add garlic; cook and stir 20 seconds. Stir in almonds and panko. Cook over medium-low to medium heat until golden. Sprinkle roasted cauliflower with almond mixture.

UP the flavor

Finish the roasted cauliflower with a squeeze of fresh lemon.

PER SERVING *175 cal., 14 g fat (5 g sat. fat), 19 mg chol., 319 mg sodium, 9 g carb., 3 g fiber, 2 g sugars, 6 g pro.*

LEMON TOASTED FARRO
AND CAULIFLOWER PILAF

Makes 10 servings

- 1 Tbsp. olive oil
- 1½ cups farro
- 3 cups water
- ½ cup chopped onion
- 1 tsp. salt
- 1 lemon
- 2 cups small cauliflower florets
- 3 cloves garlic, minced
- 1½ tsp. ground turmeric
- ¼ tsp. black pepper
- 1 Tbsp. snipped fresh thyme

DIRECTIONS

In a large heavy saucepan heat oil over medium-high heat. Add farro; cook and stir 5 to 6 minutes or until toasted with a nutty aroma. Stir in the water, onion, and salt. Bring to boiling; reduce heat. Simmer, covered, 30 minutes or just until farro is tender.

Remove 2 tsp. grated zest and 3 Tbsp. juice from lemon. Stir lemon zest, cauliflower, garlic, turmeric, and pepper into farro mixture. Cook, covered, over medium-high heat 4 minutes. Cook, uncovered, 4 minutes more or until cauliflower is tender and liquid is absorbed, stirring occasionally. Stir in lemon juice and thyme.

PER SERVING 126 cal., 2 g fat (0 g sat. fat), 0 mg chol., 241 mg sodium, 23 g carb., 4 g fiber, 1 g sugars, 4 g pro.

WARM ROASTED BARLEY, KALE, AND APPLE SALAD

Makes 4 servings

- 1¼ cups regular pearled barley
- ¼ cup olive oil
- 1 tsp. salt
- 1¼ cups apple cider
- ¾ cup water
- 6 cups torn kale leaves
- ⅓ cup snipped pitted whole dates
- 2 Tbsp. orange juice
- 2 Tbsp. cider vinegar
- 1 cup thinly sliced Braeburn or Honeycrisp apple
- ⅓ cup crumbed ricotta salata or feta cheese
- ¼ cup pistachio nuts or toasted walnuts, coarsely chopped (tip p. 20)

DIRECTIONS

Preheat oven to 375°F. In a 2- to 3-qt. casserole combine barley, 1 Tbsp. of the oil, and the salt. Roast, uncovered, 25 minutes or until well toasted, stirring occasionally.

Meanwhile, in a small saucepan bring cider and the water to boiling. Pour over barley. Roast, covered, 40 minutes or just until barley is tender. Stir in kale, dates, and orange juice. Roast, uncovered, 6 minutes more or until kale begins to soften. Stir in vinegar and remaining 3 Tbsp. oil. Serve topped with apple slices, cheese, and nuts.

BARLEY BASICS

Pearl barley has had the outer hull removed and has been polished or "pearled." It is sold in regular or quick-cooking forms.

PER SERVING *566 cal., 22 g fat (4 g sat. fat), 11 mg chol., 785 mg sodium, 85 g carb., 16 g fiber, 25 g sugars, 14 g pro.*

BAKED EGGPLANT FRIES

Makes 8 servings

Nonstick cooking spray

1   5.3- to 7-oz. container plain Greek yogurt

3   oz. feta cheese, crumbled

2   Tbsp. snipped fresh oregano

2   Tbsp. water

1   Tbsp. lemon juice

1   large eggplant (1½ lb.), peeled if desired

1½ tsp. salt

¼   tsp. black pepper

½   cup all-purpose flour

3   eggs, lightly beaten

2   cups panko bread crumbs

⅔   cup grated Parmesan cheese

¾   cup purchased olive tapenade or bruschetta topper (optional)

DIRECTIONS

Preheat oven to 450°F. Lightly coat two large baking sheets with cooking spray. For yogurt sauce, in a bowl combine the next five ingredients (through lemon juice). Cover; chill until serving.

Cut the eggplant into 3×½ to 4×½-inch sticks. Sprinkle with ½ tsp. of the salt and the pepper. Let stand 10 minutes. Blot dry with paper towels. Place flour and remaining 1 tsp. salt in a shallow dish. Place eggs in another shallow dish. In a third shallow dish combine panko and Parmesan cheese. Working in batches, place the eggplant sticks into flour, then egg, then bread crumb mixture; arrange on prepared baking sheets. Coat "fries" with cooking spray. Bake 15 minutes or until browned and crisp. (Bake the first batch while continuing to bread the second batch.) Serve with yogurt sauce and tapenade.

DIY TAPENADE

To make quick olive tapenade, toss finely chopped assorted olives and finely chopped roasted sweet red pepper with a drizzle of olive oil.

PER SERVING *187 cal., 7 g fat (3 g sat. fat), 90 mg chol., 710 mg sodium, 21 g carb., 3 g fiber, 5 g sugars, 10 g pro.*

SHAVED BRUSSELS SPROUTS
WITH GREEN ONION VINAIGRETTE

[VEGETARIAN]---[COMPANY]--

Makes 8 servings

- 4 green onions
- ¼ cup olive oil
- ¼ cup lemon juice
- 1 Tbsp. white wine vinegar
- 1 Tbsp. honey
- 1 tsp. ground coriander
- ½ tsp. kosher salt
- 1 lb. Brussels sprouts, trimmed and very thinly sliced*
- 2 oranges, peeled and sectioned
- 1 cup cashews, toasted (tip p. 20)

DIRECTIONS

For vinaigrette, chop green onions, separating white parts from green tops. In a blender or food processor combine white parts of onions and the next six ingredients (through salt). Cover and blend or process until smooth.

In a large bowl combine Brussels sprouts and green tops of onions. Pour vinaigrette over sprouts; toss gently to coat. Stir in oranges and cashews.

MAKE IT
AHEAD

Prepare the recipe as directed. Cover and chill up to 4 hours. Stir before serving.

*INGREDIENT KNOW-HOW

To trim Brussels sprouts, cut off the stems just at the spot where the leaves are attached. Remove dark green outer leaves until the tender, light green leaves are uniformly exposed. If available, use a food processor to shave Brussels sprouts, or purchase them already shaved.

PER SERVING *162 cal., 11 g fat (2 g sat. fat), 0 mg chol., 140 mg sodium, 15 g carb., 3 g fiber, 7 g sugars, 4 g pro.*

ROASTED BRUSSELS SPROUTS WITH APPLES, CHERRIES, AND PECANS

Makes 4 servings

1 lb. Brussels sprouts, trimmed and halved (tip p. 234)

2 Tbsp. olive oil

½ tsp. kosher salt

⅛ tsp. cayenne pepper

1 cup sliced or coarsely chopped apple

½ cup dried cherries or cranberries

¼ cup chopped pecans

¼ cup red wine, raspberry, or other desired vinaigrette salad dressing

DIRECTIONS

Preheat oven to 425°F. Place Brussels sprouts in a 15×10-inch baking pan. Drizzle with oil and sprinkle with salt and cayenne pepper; toss to coat.

Roast 15 minutes. Stir in apple, dried cherries, and pecans. Roast 5 to 10 minutes or until sprouts are crisp-tender and lightly browned. Drizzle with vinaigrette; toss to coat.

PER SERVING *250 cal., 15 g fat (2 g sat. fat), 0 mg chol., 389 mg sodium, 32 g carb., 6 g fiber, 18 g sugars, 5 g pro.*

BALSAMIC ROASTED BRUSSELS
SPROUTS WITH BACON

Makes 4 servings

- 1 lb. Brussels sprouts, trimmed and halved or quartered (tip p. 234)
- 2 Tbsp. balsamic vinegar
- 1 Tbsp. olive oil
- ¼ tsp. salt
- ¼ tsp. black pepper
- 2 slices bacon, crisp-cooked and crumbled
- 2 tsp. grated lemon zest (optional)

DIRECTIONS

Preheat oven to 400°F. Line a 15×10-inch baking pan with foil. Place Brussels sprouts in prepared pan. Drizzle with 1 Tbsp. of the vinegar and the oil, and sprinkle with salt and pepper; toss to coat.

Roast 15 to 20 minutes or until sprouts are crisp-tender and browned, stirring every 5 minutes. Drizzle with remaining 1 Tbsp. vinegar; sprinkle with bacon and, if desired, lemon zest.

PER SERVING *104 cal., 5 g fat (1 g sat. fat), 4 mg chol., 242 mg sodium, 12 g carb., 4 g fiber, 4 g sugars, 5 g pro.*

SHAVED CELERY AND MUSHROOM SALAD WITH PECORINO

Makes 6 servings

- 4 cups very thinly bias-sliced celery
- 4 cups thinly sliced fresh cremini mushrooms
- ½ cup coarsely snipped fresh Italian parsley
- ¼ cup olive oil
- 3 to 4 Tbsp. lemon juice
- 2 Tbsp. white wine vinegar
- 1 tsp. kosher salt
- 2 oz. Pecorino Romano cheese, shaved

DIRECTIONS

In an extra-large bowl combine celery, mushrooms, and parsley. For dressing, in a screw-top jar combine olive oil, lemon juice, and vinegar. Cover and shake well.

Drizzle dressing over salad and sprinkle with salt; toss gently to coat. Top with cheese.

MAKE IT AHEAD

Cut, slice, and combine celery, mushrooms, and parsley. Cover and chill up to 24 hours.

PER SERVING *146 cal., 12 g fat (3 g sat. fat), 10 mg chol., 561 mg sodium, 5 g carb., 2 g fiber, 3 g sugars, 6 g pro.*

TINY TOMATO SALAD WITH
CHAMPAGNE VINAIGRETTE

[VEGETARIAN] --- [HEALTHY] --- [COMPANY]

Makes 12 servings

- 2 pints assorted tiny tomatoes
- 2 cups arugula or watercress
- 1 small fennel bulb, quartered, cored, and very thinly sliced (about 1 cup) (tip p. 213)
- ⅓ cup chopped fresh Italian parsley
- ¼ cup finely chopped shallots
- ¼ cup olive oil
- 3 Tbsp. Champagne vinegar
- 1 tsp. grated lemon zest
- ¼ tsp. salt
- ⅛ tsp. black pepper

DIRECTIONS

Cut about 1 cup tomatoes in half. In a salad bowl toss together the first four ingredients (through parsley).

For vinaigrette, in a screw-top jar combine the remaining ingredients. Cover and shake well. Pour vinaigrette over tomato salad.

SWAP IT OUT

Champagne vinegar is made from the same grapes used in making Champagne: Chardonnay and Pinot. The vinegar has mild flavor with subtle sweetness. White wine vinegar is a good substitute.

PER SERVING *58 cal., 5 g fat (1 g sat. fat), 0 mg chol., 58 mg sodium, 4 g carb., 1 g fiber, 2 g sugars, 1 g pro.*

SUMMER SPAGHETTI SALAD

[VEGETARIAN] ---- [COMPANY]

Makes 10 servings

- ½ cup walnuts
- ½ cup olive oil
- 1 tsp. kosher salt
- 3 cloves garlic, sliced
- 1 12-oz. pkg. spaghetti, broken in half
- 3 cups reduced-sodium chicken broth
- 1 medium zucchini, ends trimmed
- 1 medium yellow summer squash, ends trimmed
- 6 sticks string cheese
- 4 cups chopped red and yellow cherry tomatoes
- 1 cup finely chopped onion
- 1 cup chopped fresh Italian parsley
- ½ tsp. freshly ground black pepper
- ¼ cup red wine vinegar

DIRECTIONS

Preheat oven to 350°F. In a shallow baking pan toss together walnuts, 1 tsp. of the olive oil, and ¼ tsp. of the salt. Bake 5 minutes or until walnuts are toasted. Set aside. In an extra-large skillet heat 2 Tbsp. of the oil over medium heat. Add garlic; cook and stir 1 minute. Add pasta, tossing to combine. Add broth. Cook, uncovered, over medium heat 10 minutes or until liquid is nearly absorbed, stirring occasionally. Remove from heat; cool 10 minutes. Transfer to a serving dish.

Meanwhile, use a spiral vegetable slicer to cut zucchini and yellow squash into long strands. Snip strands into shorter lengths, if desired. Add to spaghetti in dish. Let cool completely. Pull cheese into thin strands; cover and chill until ready to serve. In a small bowl toss together remaining ingredients and the remaining oil. Add cheese to spaghetti salad. Top with tomato mixture and walnuts.

PER SERVING *335 cal., 19 g fat (4 g sat. fat), 9 mg chol., 443 mg sodium, 33 g carb., 2 g fiber, 5 g sugars, 12 g pro.*

SUMMER PASTA SALAD

Makes 16 servings

- 8 oz. dried lasagna noodles, broken into 3-inch pieces, or 3 cups dried bow tie or penne pasta
- 2 Tbsp. olive oil
- 1 Tbsp. lemon juice
- 1 tsp. salt
- 1 clove garlic, minced
- 1½ cups fresh green beans, trimmed
- 8 oz. bite-size fresh mozzarella balls or cubed fresh mozzarella cheese
- 1½ cups thinly sliced yellow summer squash and/or zucchini
- 1 cup chopped tomatoes and/or halved cherry tomatoes
- 2 oz. thinly sliced prosciutto, torn into bite-size pieces, and/or salami, halved and sliced (optional)
- 1 cup arugula or fresh baby spinach
- ½ cup thinly sliced, halved red onion
- ½ cup pitted ripe olives, halved and/or pitted Kalamata olives (optional)
- 2 to 3 Tbsp. slivered fresh basil
- 1 recipe Red Wine Vinaigrette

DIRECTIONS

Cook pasta according to package directions; drain. Rinse with cold water; drain well. In an extra-large bowl whisk together the next four ingredients (through garlic). Add pasta; toss to coat. Cover; chill 8 to 24 hours.

In a large saucepan cook green beans in a large amount of boiling water 5 minutes; drain. Let cool. Add green beans and the next eight ingredients (though basil) to pasta. Drizzle with Red Wine Vinaigrette. Toss to coat. Cover; chill 4 to 24 hours.

RED WINE VINAIGRETTE
In a screw-top jar combine 1 cup olive oil; ⅓ cup red wine, white wine, rice, or cider vinegar; ¼ cup shallots, finely chopped; 2 Tbsp. snipped fresh oregano, thyme, or basil, or 1 tsp. dried oregano, thyme, or basil, crushed; 1 Tbsp. Dijon-style mustard or ½ tsp. dry mustard; 2 tsp. sugar; 2 cloves garlic, minced; ¼ tsp. salt; and ¼ tsp. black pepper. Cover; shake well.

PER SERVING 245 cal., 19 g fat (4 g sat. fat), 10 mg chol., 290 mg sodium, 14 g carb., 1 g fiber, 2 g sugars, 5 g pro.

CORN PUDDING CASSEROLE

Makes 12 servings

- 6 dried tomatoes (not oil-pack)
- ½ cup chopped onion
- 2 cloves garlic, minced
- 2 Tbsp. butter
- 1¼ cups shredded zucchini
- 1 16-oz. pkg. frozen whole kernel corn, thawed
- 6 eggs, lightly beaten
- 3 cups whole milk
- ¾ cup yellow cornmeal
- 1 15-oz. carton whole milk ricotta cheese
- 2 tsp. dried Italian seasoning, crushed
- 1 tsp. salt
- ¼ tsp. black pepper
- 1 cup finely shredded Parmesan cheese (4 oz.)
- 1 cup panko
- 1 Tbsp. butter, melted
- Chopped fresh Italian parsley (optional)

DIRECTIONS

Preheat oven to 350°F. Grease a 3-qt. baking dish; set aside. In a small bowl cover tomatoes with boiling water. Let stand 15 minutes; drain. Chop tomatoes; set aside. Meanwhile, in a large skillet cook onion and garlic in 2 Tbsp. hot butter over medium heat 4 minutes or until tender. Add zucchini; cook 2 minutes more. Stir in corn and chopped tomatoes; set aside.

In a large bowl whisk together eggs and milk. Gradually whisk in cornmeal. Whisk in ricotta cheese, Italian seasoning, salt, and pepper. Stir in the corn mixture and Parmesan cheese. Pour into prepared dish (dish will be full). Bake 20 minutes. Meanwhile, in a bowl toss together panko and 1 Tbsp. melted butter. Sprinkle on casserole. Bake 30 minutes or until the top is browned and a knife inserted into center comes out clean. If desired, sprinkle with parsley.

MAKE IT AHEAD

Prepare as directed, except do not preheat oven. Cool zucchini mixture to room temperature; stir in corn and tomatoes. Proceed as directed up to the point of baking. Cover dish tightly with foil; chill up to 24 hours. Stir corn mixture. Top with panko mixture. Bake and top as directed.

PER SERVING *279 cal., 14 g fat (8 g sat. fat), 142 mg chol., 455 mg sodium, 24 g carb., 2 g fiber, 6 g sugars, 15 g pro.*

CRISPY PARMESAN-ROASTED BUTTERNUT SQUASH

Makes 4 servings

Nonstick cooking spray

1 1½- to 1¾-lb. butternut squash, peeled, seeded, and cut into ¾-inch pieces

2 Tbsp. olive oil

½ tsp. kosher salt

⅛ tsp. black pepper

⅓ cup grated Parmesan cheese

¼ tsp. dried thyme, sage, or basil, crushed

DIRECTIONS

Preheat oven to 425°F. Coat a 15×10-inch baking pan with cooking spray. Place squash in prepared pan. Drizzle with oil and sprinkle with salt and pepper; toss to coat.

Roast 15 minutes. Stir squash; roast 5 minutes more. Stir in cheese and thyme. Roast 5 minutes or until squash is tender.

UP the flavor

Drizzle the roasted squash with a little balsamic vinegar right before serving.

PER SERVING *154 cal., 9 g fat (2 g sat. fat), 6 mg chol., 267 mg sodium, 18 g carb., 3 g fiber, 3 g sugars, 3 g pro.*

MASHED SWEET POTATOES
WITH MUSHOOMS AND BACON

Makes 10 servings

6   slices bacon,
    chopped

8   oz. cremini
    mushrooms, halved
    (quartered if large)

1   medium red
    onion, cut into thin
    wedges

2   Tbsp. lemon juice

⅓   cup golden raisins

3   lb. orange-flesh
    sweet potatoes,
    peeled and cut into
    1½-inch pieces

½   cup milk

2   Tbsp. butter

1   tsp. kosher salt

DIRECTIONS

In a 6-qt. pot cook bacon over medium heat 8 to 10 minutes or until crisp. Drain bacon on paper towels, reserving 3 Tbsp. drippings in pot. Add mushrooms and onion to drippings. Cook and stir over medium heal 8 minutes or until mushrooms are tender and browned. Drizzle with lemon juice. Stir cooked bacon and raisins into mushroom mixture. Transfer to a bowl; cover to keep warm.

Wipe out the pot. Add sweet potatoes and enough salted water to cover. Bring to boiling. Cook potatoes, covered, 20 to 25 minutes or until tender. Drain; return to pot. Using a potato masher or fork, mash potatoes. Stir in milk, butter, and salt until butter is melted. Stir in mushroom mixture or, if desired, stir in half the mushroom mixture and top with remaining half.

MAKE
IT AHEAD

Prepare as directed, stirring all of the mushroom mixture into mashed sweet potatoes. Transfer mixture to a storage container; cover and chill up to 24 hours. To serve, return sweet potatoes to the pot; heat through.

PER SERVING *226 cal., 8 g fat (4 g sat. fat), 15 mg chol., 379 mg sodium, 34 g carb., 5 g fiber, 10 g sugars, 5 g pro.*

BASIL AND OLIVE POTATOES

Makes 10 servings

2	lb. small new potatoes, quartered
⅓	cup canola oil
1½	cups fresh basil leaves
3	cloves garlic, minced
⅓	cup white wine vinegar
2	Tbsp. lemon juice
2	Tbsp. mayonnaise
½	tsp. salt
½	tsp. black pepper
2	large yellow sweet peppers
1	cup pitted green olives

DIRECTIONS

In a large pot cook potatoes in boiling salted water, covered, 10 minutes or just until tender; drain. Meanwhile, for dressing, in a small saucepan combine oil, ½ cup of the basil, and the garlic; cook over medium-low heat 5 minutes. Remove and discard basil from oil. In a blender combine garlic oil and the next five ingredients (through black pepper). Cover and blend until smooth. Transfer potatoes to a serving bowl. Pour dressing over potatoes; gently toss to coat. Cover and set aside.

Grill sweet peppers, covered, over medium heat 7 to 10 minutes or until charred, turning occasionally. Cool slightly. Halve peppers; remove stems and seeds. Cut into large pieces. Add grilled pepper pieces and olives to potatoes; toss to coat. Add the remaining basil and toss again. Serve warm or at room temperature.

PER SERVING 180 cal., 11 g fat (1 g sat. fat), 1 mg chol., 305 mg sodium, 19 g carb., 3 g fiber, 2 g sugars, 2 g pro.

ROASTED SAGE
FINGERLING POTATOES

Makes 6 servings

15 fingerling potatoes and/or small new potatoes, halved lengthwise

2 Tbsp. olive oil

¼ tsp. hickory smoked salt or seasoned salt

30 fresh sage leaves

DIRECTIONS

Preheat oven to 425°F. Line a baking sheet with parchment paper. In a medium bowl combine potatoes, oil, and salt; toss to coat. Press a sage leaf against cut side of each potato half. Arrange potatoes, cut sides down, on prepared baking sheet.

Roast 15 to 20 minutes or until potatoes are tender. Serve warm or at room temperature.

PER SERVING *114 cal., 6 g fat (0 g sat. fat), 0 mg chol., 84 mg sodium, 18 g carb., 0 g fiber, 0 g sugars, 0 g pro.*

MASHED POTATOES WITH GOUDA

Makes 8 servings

- 2 green onions
- 5 oz. pancetta, cut into ¼-inch cubes (about 1 cup)
- 1 lb. red potatoes, cut into 1½-inch pieces
- 1 lb. russet potatoes, peeled and cut into 1½-inch pieces
- ¾ cup half-and-half or heavy cream
- 2 cups finely shredded Gouda cheese (8 oz.)
  Salt
  Freshly ground black pepper

DIRECTIONS

Thinly slice white portions of green onions. Bias-slice green onion tops and set aside for serving. In a 4-qt. pot cook white portions of onions and the pancetta over medium-high heat about 8 minutes or until pancetta is crisp, stirring occasionally. Remove and set aside. Drain off fat. In the same pot cook potatoes, covered, in enough lightly salted boiling water to cover 20 to 25 minutes or until tender; drain. Return potatoes to pot.

Add half-and-half to cooked potatoes. Mash with a potato masher or mixer on low until nearly smooth. Stir in 1½ cups of the cheese and the pancetta mixture. Season to taste with salt and pepper. Transfer mashed potatoes to a serving dish. Sprinkle with the remaining ½ cup cheese, green onion tops, and, if desired, additional crisp-cooked pancetta.

MAKE IT AHEAD

Prepare as directed except transfer mashed potatoes to a greased 2-qt. baking dish. Cover with foil; chill up to 24 hours. Bake at 350°F for 40 minutes or until heated through. Remove foil. Top as directed.

PER SERVING 272 cal., 16 g fat (9 g sat. fat), 47 mg chol., 502 mg sodium, 21 g carb., 2 g fiber, 2 g sugars, 13 g pro.

ROASTED SMASHED POTATOES

VEGETARIAN · COMPANY

Makes 6 servings

12 to 16 small red
    potatoes (1½ to
    2 inches in
    diameter)

1 tsp. salt

¼ cup olive oil

¾ tsp. salt

½ tsp. black pepper

¾ cup finely shredded
    Parmesan cheese
    (3 oz.)

2 Tbsp. finely
    snipped fresh
    Italian parsley

DIRECTIONS

In a large saucepan cook potatoes with 1 tsp. salt, covered, in enough boiling water to cover 25 to 30 minutes or until very tender; drain. Preheat oven to 450°F. Line a 15×10-inch baking pan with foil. Transfer potatoes to prepared pan; cool 10 minutes. Using a potato masher or the palm of your hand, lightly press each potato to smash to ½-inch thickness, keeping potato in one piece. Brush with half the oil and sprinkle with half the ¾ tsp. salt and ¼ tsp. of the pepper.

Roast 10 to 15 minutes or until bottoms are light brown and crisp. Turn potatoes; brush with remaining oil and sprinkle with remaining salt and pepper. Roast 10 to 15 minutes more or until potatoes are light brown and crisp. In a small bowl combine cheese and parsley; sprinkle over potatoes. Roast 2 to 3 minutes or until cheese is melted.

PER SERVING *202 cal., 12 g fat (2 g sat. fat), 8 mg chol., 514 mg sodium, 18 g carb., 2 g fiber, 2 g sugars, 6 g pro.*

EASY SESAME DINNER ROLLS

{ VEGETARIAN } - { HEALTHY } - { COMPANY }

Makes 16 servings

1   16-oz. loaf frozen white or wheat bread dough

¼   cup sesame seeds

2   Tbsp. yellow cornmeal

2   Tbsp. grated Parmesan cheese

1   tsp. salt-free lemon-pepper seasoning

3   Tbsp. butter, melted

DIRECTIONS

Thaw dough according to package directions. Grease a 9-inch square baking pan; set aside. In a shallow dish or small bowl stir together sesame seeds, cornmeal, Parmesan cheese, and lemon-pepper seasoning. Place butter in a second dish. Cut the dough into 16 equal pieces. Shape each piece into a ball by pulling and pinching dough underneath.

Roll dough pieces in butter, then in the sesame seed mixture to lightly coat. Arrange dough pieces, smooth sides up, in the prepared pan. Cover pan with waxed paper. Let rise in a warm place until nearly double in size (45 to 60 minutes). Preheat oven to 375°F. Bake 25 minutes or until golden brown. Transfer rolls to a wire rack. Cool slightly before serving.

GARLIC-HERB ROLLS

Prepare as directed except omit lemon-pepper seasoning, and add 1 tsp. dried Italian seasoning (crushed) and ½ tsp. garlic powder to sesame seed mixture.

PER SERVING *109 cal., 4 g fat (2 g sat. fat), 6 mg chol., 180 mg sodium, 15 g carb., 1 g fiber, 1 g sugars, 2 g pro.*

TOASTED MILLET NO-KNEAD WHOLE WHEAT ROLLS

Makes 24 servings

- 2 cups whole wheat flour
- 5 Tbsp. yellow cornmeal
- 2 pkg. active dry yeast
- 1½ tsp. salt
- ½ cup millet
- 2 cups milk
- ⅓ cup butter, cut up
- 2 eggs
- 3 Tbsp. molasses
- 2 to 2½ cups all-purpose flour
- 2 Tbsp. butter, melted

DIRECTIONS

In a large bowl stir together whole wheat flour, 4 Tbsp. of the cornmeal, the yeast, and salt. In a large saucepan cook millet over medium heat 5 minutes or until toasted with a nutty aroma, stirring occasionally. Add milk and the ⅓ cup butter. Heat and stir just until warm (120°F to 130°F) and butter is almost melted. Add milk mixture to yeast mixture; add eggs and molasses. Beat with a mixer on low 30 seconds, scraping bowl constantly. Beat on high 3 minutes. Stir in as much of the all-purpose flour as you can to make a soft yet firm dough. Cover and let rise in a warm place until double in size (45 to 60 minutes). Lightly grease a 13×9-inch baking pan.

Punch dough down; turn out onto a floured surface. Using floured hands, press dough into an 11×7-inch rectangle. Cut into 24 pieces; transfer to prepared pan. Cover and let rise in a warm place until double in size (30 to 40 minutes). Preheat oven to 400°F. Brush rolls with melted butter and sprinkle with remaining 1 Tbsp. cornmeal. Bake 25 minutes or until rolls are golden and sound hollow when lightly tapped. Cool in pan 10 minutes. Pull apart and serve warm.

MAKE IT AHEAD

To freeze, let rolls cool completely. Wrap in foil and freeze in a resealable plastic bag up to 3 months. To reheat, thaw at room temperature. Warm rolls, wrapped in foil, in a 350°F oven for 15 minutes.

PER SERVING *151 cal., 5 g fat (3 g sat. fat), 26 mg chol., 191 mg sodium, 23 g carb., 2 g fiber, 3 g sugars, 4 g pro.*

SWEET POTATO DINNER BISCUITS

[WEEKNIGHT] --- [VEGETARIAN] --- [COMPANY]

Makes 12 servings

2½ cups all-purpose flour

1 Tbsp. baking powder

1½ tsp. salt

⅓ cup shortening, chilled

1 cup mashed sweet potato*

¾ cup milk

DIRECTIONS

Preheat oven to 425°F. In a large bowl stir together flour, baking powder, and salt. Use a pastry blender to cut in shortening until mixture resembles coarse crumbs. In a bowl combine mashed sweet potato and milk. Use a fork to gradually stir sweet potato mixture into flour mixture. Do not overmix. Turn dough out onto a floured surface. Knead dough by folding and gently pressing just until dough holds together.

Roll or pat dough into an 8×6-inch rectangle. Cut with a floured 2-inch round cutter or use a knife to cut into 2-inch squares; reroll scraps as needed and dip cutter into flour between cuts. Place 1 inch apart on an ungreased baking sheet. Bake 12 to 14 minutes or until golden. Serve warm.

*MASHED SWEET POTATO
Prick one 12-oz. sweet potato in several places with a fork. Microwave 6 to 7 minutes or until very tender. When cool enough to handle, scrape flesh from potato. (You can also use one 15-oz. can sweet potatoes, drained.) Mash sweet potato and measure 1 cup.

PER SERVING 174 cal., 6 g fat (2 g sat. fat), 1 mg chol., 428 mg sodium, 26 g carb., 1 g fiber, 2 g sugars, 4 g pro.

SALTED PECAN AND ORANGE SCONES

Makes 12 servings

1 orange
2½ cups all-purpose flour
2 Tbsp. packed brown sugar
1 Tbsp. baking powder
¼ tsp. salt
6 Tbsp. butter, cut up
1 egg, lightly beaten
¾ cup heavy cream
1 cup salted, toasted pecan halves
½ cup powdered sugar
Orange zest strips (optional)

DIRECTIONS

Line a baking sheet with parchment paper; set aside. Remove 2¼ tsp. grated zest and 1 Tbsp. juice from orange; set aside. Preheat oven to 400°F. In a large bowl combine flour, brown sugar, baking powder, and salt. Using a pastry blender, cut in butter until mixture resembles coarse crumbs. Make a well in the center of flour mixture; set aside.

In a medium bowl combine egg, cream, and 2 tsp. of the orange zest. Add egg mixture all at once to flour mixture. Add pecans. Using a fork, stir just until moistened. Turn dough out onto a lightly floured surface. Knead dough by folding and gently pressing 10 to 12 strokes or until dough is nearly smooth. Pat into a 10×4-inch rectangle. Cut in half lengthwise and in sixths crosswise to make 12 rectangles. Place rectangles 2 inches apart on prepared baking sheet. Brush wedges with additional cream.

Bake 13 to 15 minutes or until golden brown. Remove scones from baking sheet; cool slightly. Meanwhile, for the orange glaze, in a bowl stir together powdered sugar, remaining ¼ tsp. orange zest, and the orange juice. Drizzle or brush scones with orange glaze. If desired, sprinkle with orange peel strips. Serve warm.

SALTED, TOASTED PECANS

Toss 1 cup raw pecan halves with 2 tsp. olive oil and ½ tsp. salt. Spread in a shallow baking pan. Bake at 350°F for 5 to 8 minutes or until toasted, stirring once. Cool.

PER SERVING *309 cal., 20 g fat (8 g sat. fat), 55 mg chol., 266 mg sodium, 29 g carb., 2 g fiber, 8 g sugars, 5 g pro.*

PEPPERED BACON, GREEN ONION, AND BUTTERMILK SCONES

Makes 26 servings

- 6 slices peppered bacon
- ½ cup finely chopped green onions
- 1 cup buttermilk or sour milk*
- 1 egg, lightly beaten
- 3 cups all-purpose flour
- 1 Tbsp. baking powder
- ¼ tsp. garlic powder
- ¼ tsp. cayenne pepper
- ½ cup butter, cut up
- 1½ cups finely shredded Gruyère cheese (6 oz.)

DIRECTIONS

Preheat oven to 425°F. In an extra-large skillet cook bacon over medium heat until crisp. Drain bacon on paper towels. Crumble bacon; set aside. Discard all but 2 Tbsp. drippings from skillet. Cook green onions in hot drippings until tender. Line a large baking sheet with parchment paper.

In a bowl whisk together buttermilk and egg. In another bowl combine flour, baking powder, garlic powder, and cayenne pepper. Using a pastry blender, cut in butter until mixture resembles coarse crumbs. Stir in crumbled bacon, green onions, and cheese. Make a well in the center of the flour mixture. Reserve 2 Tbsp. of the buttermilk mixture. Add remaining buttermilk mixture all at once to flour mixture. Using a fork, stir just until mixture is moistened. Turn dough out onto a lightly floured surface. Knead dough by folding and gently pressing 10 to 12 strokes or just until dough holds together.

Roll out dough evenly to ½-inch thickness. Using a 2- to 2½-inch round cutter, cut rounds from dough. Place rounds, nearly touching, on prepared baking sheet. Brush rounds with reserved 2 Tbsp. buttermilk mixture. Bake 15 minutes or until golden brown. Transfer scones to wire racks; cool completely.

*SOUR MILK
To make 1 cup sour milk, place 1 tablespoon lemon juice or vinegar in a glass measuring cup. Add enough milk to make 1 cup total liquid; stir. Let the mixture stand for 5 minutes before using.

PER SERVING *137 cal., 8 g fat (4 g sat. fat), 27 mg chol., 155 mg sodium, 12 g carb., 0 g fiber, 1 g sugars, 5 g pro.*

BACON CORN BREAD

Makes 8 servings

- ⅓ cup butter
- ¾ cup milk
- 2 eggs, lightly beaten
- ½ cup frozen whole kernel corn
- 1 cup yellow cornmeal
- ¾ cup all-purpose flour
- ⅓ cup sugar
- 1 Tbsp. baking powder
- ¾ tsp. salt
- 1 2.8- to 3-oz. pkg. cooked bacon pieces (⅔ cup)
- ¾ to 1 cup shredded cheddar cheese (3 to 4 oz.)

DIRECTIONS

Preheat oven to 350°F. In an oven-safe 3½- or 4-qt. nonstick Dutch oven melt butter over medium heat. Immediately remove pot from heat. Add milk, eggs, and corn to butter in pot; stir to combine. Add the next five ingredients (through salt). Stir just until moistened (batter should be lumpy).

Stir in half the bacon pieces and ½ cup of the cheese. Sprinkle remaining bacon and cheese over top. Bake 20 to 25 minutes or until a toothpick comes out clean. Serve warm.

SIZE IT RIGHT

To ensure accurate bake times for this recipe, check the diameter of your Dutch oven. It should be between 7½ and 8½ inches.

PER SERVING *327 cal., 16 g fat (8 g sat. fat), 87 mg chol., 865 mg sodium, 35 g carb., 1 g fiber, 10 g sugars, 12 g pro.*

PAELLA-STYLE STUFFING

Makes 8 servings

2 Tbsp. canola oil

⅓ cup chopped onion

3 garlic cloves, minced

⅔ cup short grain rice

1⅓ cups reduced-sodium chicken broth

¼ tsp. saffron threads

6 oz. smoked chorizo sausage, diced

¾ cup chopped red sweet pepper

½ cup thinly sliced celery

2 Tbsp. snipped fresh parsley

¼ tsp. salt

¼ tsp. black pepper

6 cups dried French bread cubes*

½ cup sliced pimiento-stuffed green olives

1¼ cups reduced-sodium chicken broth

DIRECTIONS

Preheat oven to 350°F. Lightly grease a 2-qt. baking dish (the bottom diameter should be 7½ to 8½ inches.) In a small saucepan heat 1 Tbsp. of the oil over medium-high heat. Add onion; cook and stir 3 minutes or until onion is tender. Add garlic; cook and stir 30 seconds more. Add rice; cook and stir 3 minutes or just until rice starts to brown. Carefully add the 1⅓ cups broth and the saffron threads. Bring to boiling; reduce heat. Cook, covered, 15 minutes or until rice is cooked and liquid is absorbed.

Meanwhile, in a large skillet heat the remaining 1 Tbsp. oil. Add chorizo, sweet pepper, and celery; cook and stir 4 minutes or until chorizo begins to brown and vegetables are tender. Remove from heat. Add rice mixture, parsley, salt, and black pepper to skillet; toss to combine. In a large bowl combine rice mixture, bread cubes, and olives. Toss to combine. Drizzle with the 1¼ cups broth to moisten; toss to combine. Spoon stuffing into prepared dish. Cover with foil. Bake 25 to 30 minutes or until heated through.

*INGREDIENT KNOW-HOW

To make dry bread cubes, preheat oven to 300°F. Cut an 8-oz. loaf of French bread into ¾-inch cubes (6 cups). Spread on a 15×10-inch baking pan. Bake 10 to 15 minutes or until dry, stirring twice; cool. (Cubes will continue to dry and crisp as they cool.) Or let bread cubes stand, loosely covered, at room temperature 8 to 12 hours.

SPICE SWAP

Saffron gives this stuffing a gentle yellow hue and distinctly warm, savory flavor. It also happens to be considered the most expensive spice on the market. If you prefer, you can use turmeric instead.

PER SERVING *408 cal., 19 g fat (5 g sat. fat), 240 mg chol., 1,067 mg sodium, 43 g carb., 3 g fiber, 3 g sugars, 15 g pro.*

DESS

SERT

Enjoy something sweet—and simplify the process of making it—with these recipes for rich rice and bread puddings, perfectly poached fruits, and silky custards and cheesecake.

CIDER-POACHED PEARS

Makes 4 servings

- 4 medium ripe yet firm pears
- 2 cups apple cider
- ¼ cup honey
- 1 3-inch cinnamon stick
- 1 Tbsp. chopped crystallized ginger
- 2 green cardamom pods, crushed to release seeds
- ½ cup vanilla-flavor Greek yogurt
- 2 Tbsp. chopped pistachios

DIRECTIONS

Core each pear from the bottom, leaving the stem intact. Peel pears. If necessary, slice the bottoms off pears to allow them to stand upright. Prepare as directed for desired cooker, below.

FAST 5-MINUTE COOK TIME

In a 4- to 6-qt. electric or stove-top pressure cooker stir together the next five ingredients (through cardamom) until honey is dissolved. Add pears to cooker. Lock lid in place. Set an electric cooker on high pressure to cook 5 minutes. For a stove-top cooker, bring up to pressure over medium-high heat; reduce heat enough to maintain steady pressure. Cook 5 minutes. Remove from heat.

For both models, release pressure quickly. Carefully open lid. Using a slotted spoon, transfer pears to dessert plates, reserving cider mixture in cooker. For an electric cooker, use the saute setting to boil gently, uncovered, 12 to 15 minutes or until syrupy. For a stove-top cooker, cook directly in the pot over medium heat. Cool slightly. Strain through a fine-mesh sieve; discard spices. Spoon cider syrup over pears. Serve with yogurt and pistachios.

SLOW 2-HOUR COOK TIME

In a 3½- or 4-qt. slow cooker stir together the next five ingredients (through cardamom) until honey is dissolved. Add pears to cooker. Cover and cook on high 2 hours or just until pears are tender. Using a slotted spoon, transfer pears to dessert plates. Transfer cooking liquid to a small saucepan; bring to boiling. Boil gently, uncovered, 12 to 15 minutes or until syrupy. Cool slightly. Strain through a fine-mesh sieve; discard spices. Spoon cider syrup over pears. Serve with yogurt and pistachios.

THE NICE SPICE

Cardamom pods contain tiny seeds that have a warm fragrance and flavor with notes of mint and lemony eucalyptus. Find them in well-stocked grocery stores, Indian grocery stores, and spice shops.

PER SERVING *204 cal, 3 g fat (1 g sat. fat), 1 mg chol., 43 mg sodium, 44 g carb, 6 g fiber, 32 g sugars, 4 g pro.*

COCONUT RICE PUDDING WITH BERRIES

[VEGETARIAN]---[COMPANY]

Makes 12 servings

Nonstick cooking spray (slow cooker only)

4 cups whole milk

2 cups full-fat unsweetened coconut milk

2 cups uncooked long grain white or jasmine rice

2 cups fresh or frozen (thawed) blueberries or raspberries

¼ cup honey or maple syrup

2 tsp. vanilla

⅔ cup shredded coconut, toasted (tip p. 20)

⅓ cup sliced almonds, toasted (tip p. 20)

FAST *10-MINUTE COOK TIME*

In a 6-qt. electric or stove-top pressure cooker combine whole milk, coconut milk, and rice. Lock lid in place. Set an electric cooker on high pressure to cook 10 minutes. For a stove-top cooker, bring up to pressure over medium-high heat; reduce heat enough to maintain steady pressure. Cook 10 minutes. Remove from heat.

For both models, let stand 15 minutes to release pressure naturally. Release remaining pressure. Carefully open lid. Gently fold in berries, honey, and vanilla. If desired, stir in additional coconut milk. Serve pudding warm topped with coconut, almonds, and additional berries.

SLOW *3-HOUR LOW OR 1½-HOUR HIGH COOK TIME*

Lightly coat a 3½- or 4-qt. slow cooker with cooking spray. In the cooker combine whole milk, coconut milk, and rice. Cover and cook on low 3 to 3½ hours or high 1½ hours or until rice is tender, stirring toward the end of cooking. Gently fold in berries, honey, and vanilla. If desired, stir in additional coconut milk. Serve pudding warm topped with coconut, almonds, and additional berries.

WARMING LEFTOVERS

To reheat the rice pudding, add 2 to 4 Tbsp. coconut milk or whole milk to one serving. Microwave 2 to 3 minutes or until heated through, stirring once halfway through heating.

PER ⅔ CUP *327 cal., 14 g fat (10 g sat. fat), 8 mg chol., 78 mg sodium, 43 g carb, 2 g fiber, 16 g sugars, 6 g pro.*

CARAMEL-GINGER
WILD RICE PUDDING

Makes 12 servings

Nonstick cooking spray

4 cups refrigerated coconut milk

1 cup uncooked wild rice, rinsed and drained

¾ cup uncooked long grain brown rice

⅓ cup sugar

2 Tbsp. butter, cut up

1 tsp. ground ginger

1 Tbsp. grated fresh ginger

Purchased caramel sauce

Chopped crystallized ginger

FAST *20-MINUTE COOK TIME*

Lightly coat a 4-qt. electric or stove-top pressure cooker with cooking spray; add milk, rices, sugar, butter, and ground ginger. Lock lid in place. Set an electric cooker on high pressure to cook 20 minutes. For a stove-top cooker, bring up to pressure over medium-high heat; reduce heat enough to maintain steady pressure. Cook 20 minutes. Remove from heat.

For both models, let stand 15 minutes to release pressure naturally. Release any remaining pressure. Carefully open lid. Stir in fresh ginger. If desired, stir in additional coconut milk. Serve pudding warm topped with caramel sauce and crystallized ginger.

SLOW *4-HOUR LOW OR 2½-HOUR HIGH COOK TIME*

Lightly coat a 3½- or 4-qt. slow cooker with cooking spray; add coconut milk, rices, sugar, butter, and ground ginger. Cover and cook on low 4 to 4½ hours or high 2½ hours or until rice is tender, stirring toward end of cooking. Stir in fresh ginger. If desired, stir in additional coconut milk. Serve pudding warm topped with caramel sauce and crystallized ginger.

CANDIED GINGER

Crystallized ginger is fresh ginger that has been candied—cooked in sugar syrup then dried. It's sweet with a spicy ginger flavor and chewy texture. Look for it in the baking or bulk aisle.

PER ⅔ CUP *254 cal., 5 g fat (4 g sat. fat), 6 mg chol., 94 mg sodium, 49 g carb., 2 g fiber, 21 g sugars, 3 g pro.*

CHOCOLATE-CHERRY BREAD PUDDING

{ VEGETARIAN }---{ COMPANY }---

Makes 6 servings

Nonstick cooking spray

1 cup fat-free milk

½ cup refrigerated or frozen egg product, thawed, or 2 eggs, lightly beaten

¼ cup granulated sugar

¼ tsp. almond extract

⅛ tsp. salt

3 cups dried whole wheat bread cubes (tip p. 274)

2 oz. bittersweet chocolate, chopped

⅓ cup dried tart cherries

3 Tbsp. powdered sugar

2 Tbsp. low-fat Greek yogurt

3 Tbsp. sliced almonds, toasted (tip p. 20) (optional)

DIRECTIONS

Lightly coat a 1-qt. round ceramic or glass baking dish with cooking spray. Cut three double-thick, 18×3-inch heavy foil strips. Crisscross strips and place dish on top of crisscross. In a large bowl combine the next five ingredients (through salt). Stir in bread cubes, chocolate, and cherries. Pour into prepared dish; cover with foil. Prepare as directed for desired cooker, below.

FAST *15-MINUTE COOK TIME*

Place a steam rack in a 6-qt. electric or stove-top pressure cooker. Add 1 cup warm water to pot. Use foil strips to place dish on steam rack. Fold strips inside pot. Lock lid in place. Set an electric cooker on high pressure to cook 15 minutes. For a stove-top cooker, bring up to pressure over medium-high heat; reduce heat enough to maintain steady pressure. Cook 15 minutes. Remove from heat.

For both models, let stand 15 minutes to release pressure naturally. Release any remaining pressure. Carefully open lid. Use foil strips to lift dish out of cooker. Cool, uncovered, on a wire rack 30 minutes.

Meanwhile, for icing, in a bowl stir together powdered sugar and yogurt. Drizzle bread pudding with icing and, if desired, sprinkle with almonds.

SLOW *3-HOUR COOK TIME*

Pour 1 cup warm water into a 3½- to 5-qt. slow cooker. Use foil strips to place dish on rack. Fold strips inside pot. Cover and cook on low 3 to 3½ hours or until a knife inserted in pudding comes out clean. Use foil strips to remove dish from cooker. Cool, uncovered, on a wire rack 30 minutes.

Meanwhile, for icing, in a bowl stir together powdered sugar and yogurt. Drizzle bread pudding with icing and, if desired, sprinkle with almonds.

PER SERVING *194 cal., 4 g fat (2 g sat. fat), 2 mg chol., 184 mg sodium, 34 g carb., 2 g fiber, 25 g sugars, 7 g pro.*

TIRAMISU CHOCOLATE
MARBLE CAKE

Makes 8 servings

Nonstick spray for baking

½ cup butter, softened

½ cup sugar

½ tsp. baking powder

¼ tsp. salt

2 eggs

1 tsp. vanilla

½ cup all-purpose flour

¼ cup mascarpone cheese, softened

2 Tbsp. boiling water

1 Tbsp. instant espresso coffee powder

2 oz. bittersweet or semisweet chocolate, melted and cooled slightly

1 recipe Mascarpone Icing

DIRECTIONS

Generously coat a 3-cup fluted tube pan with baking spray. In a bowl beat butter with a mixer on medium 30 seconds. Add sugar, baking powder, and salt. Beat on medium 1 to 2 minutes more or until well combined. Add eggs, one at a time, beating well after each addition. Beat in vanilla. Add flour; beat just until combined. In another bowl beat mascarpone cheese until smooth. Spoon half the batter into mascarpone cheese. Beat just until combined. In another bowl whisk together boiling water and espresso powder until dissolved. Add to remaining plain batter. Stir in melted chocolate. Alternately drop spoonfuls of chocolate and mascarpone batters into prepared pan. Using a table knife, gently cut through batters to swirl them together (do not overmix). Prepare as directed for desired cooker, below.

FAST   *25-MINUTE COOK TIME*

Place a steam rack in a 6-qt. electric or stove-top pressure cooker. Add 1 cup water to pot. Set cake pan on rack. Lock lid in place. Set an electric cooker on high pressure to cook 25 minutes. For a stove-top cooker, bring up to pressure over medium-high heat; reduce heat enough to maintain steady pressure. Cook 25 minutes. Remove from heat. For both models, quickly release pressure. Carefully open lid. Carefully remove pan from cooker. Cool cake in pan on a wire rack 10 minutes. Invert cake on wire rack; cool completely. Drizzle Mascarpone Icing over cooled cake.

SLOW   *2½-HOUR HIGH COOK TIME*

Pour 1 cup water into a 5- to 6-qt. slow cooker. Set cake pan in cooker. Place a dish towel over top of cooker; add lid. Cook on high 2½ to 3 hours or until a toothpick inserted near center comes out clean. Carefully remove cake from cooker. Cool cake in pan on a wire rack 10 minutes. Invert cake on wire rack; cool completely. Drizzle Mascarpone Icing over cooled cake.

MASCARPONE ICING

In a bowl beat 2 Tbsp. softened mascarpone cheese with a mixer on medium 30 seconds. Add 1 tsp. milk and 1 tsp. amaretto; beat until smooth. Gradually beat in ⅔ cup powdered sugar until smooth. Gradually beat in 2 to 3 tsp. milk, 1 tsp. at a time, until icing is drizzling consistency.

TIP

A pressure cooker produces a moist and tender dense cake, much like a steamed cake. A slow cooker cake will have a fine texture typical of a traditionally baked cake.

PER SERVING *326 cal, 20 g fat (12 g sat. fat), 92 mg chol., 218 mg sodium, 34 g carb., 1 g fiber, 26 g sugars, 3 g pro.*

MINI CHOCOLATE-ORANGE
MOLTEN LAVA CAKES

Makes 4 servings

- 6 oz. bittersweet chocolate, chopped
- ½ cup butter
- ½ cup granulated sugar
- ¼ tsp. salt
- 3 eggs, lightly beaten
- 1 Tbsp. orange liqueur or orange juice
- 1 tsp. vanilla
- ¼ cup all-purpose flour
- 1 tsp. grated orange zest

  Powdered sugar (optional)

DIRECTIONS

Grease four 5- to 6-oz. ramekins. In a medium microwave-safe bowl melt chocolate and butter on 50% power 1 to 2 minutes, stirring every 20 seconds. Stir in sugar and salt. Whisk in eggs, orange liqueur, and vanilla. Fold in flour and orange zest. Spoon batter into ramekins. Cover dishes with foil. Prepare as directed for desired cooker, below.

FAST   9-MINUTE COOK TIME

Place a steam rack in a 6-qt. electric or stove-top pressure cooker. Add 1 cup water to pot. Place three ramekins on steam rack; stagger remaining ramekin on top. Lock lid in place. Set an electric cooker on high pressure to cook 9 minutes. For a stove-top cooker, bring up to pressure over medium-high heat; reduce heat enough to maintain steady pressure. Cook 9 minutes. Remove from heat.

For both models, release pressure quickly. Carefully open lid. Let ramekins stand in cooker 10 minutes. Remove ramekins from cooker. Serve warm. If desired, dust with powdered sugar and sprinkle with additional orange zest just before serving.

SLOW   1¾-HOUR LOW COOK TIME

Pour 2 cups water into a 5- to 6-qt. slow cooker (about ½-inch up sides of cooker). Carefully arrange filled ramekins in water in the cooker. Cover and cook on low 1¾ to 2 hours or just until cakes are set. Remove lid. Let ramekins stand in cooker 10 minutes. Carefully remove ramekins from cooker. Serve warm. If desired, dust with powdered sugar and sprinkle with additional orange zest just before serving.

PER SERVING 624 cal., 44 g fat (26 g sat. fat), 201 mg chol., 382 mg sodium, 56 g carb., 3 g fiber, 43 g sugars, 9 g pro.

AZTEC POTS DE CRÈME

Makes 5 servings

1½ cups heavy cream

2½ oz. semisweet chocolate, chopped

¼ tsp. ground cinnamon

⅛ tsp. cayenne pepper

4 egg yolks

3 Tbsp. sugar

1 tsp. vanilla

¼ tsp. salt

1 recipe Cinnamon-Sugar Pepitas

DIRECTIONS

In a medium saucepan heat and stir ¼ cup of the cream and the chocolate over low heat until chocolate is melted. Remove from heat. Gradually whisk in remaining 1¼ cups cream, the cinnamon, and cayenne pepper. In a large bowl whisk together egg yolks, sugar, vanilla, and salt. Gradually whisk cream mixture into egg yolk mixture. Ladle the custard into five 4-oz. ramekins. Prepare as directed for desired cooker, below.

FAST *10-MINUTE COOK TIME*

Carefully cover ramekins with foil. Place a steam rack in a 6-qt. electric or stove-top pressure cooker. Add 1½ cups hot water to pot. Place three ramekins on steam rack; stagger remaining two ramekins on top. Lock lid in place. Set an electric cooker on high pressure to cook 10 minutes. For a stove-top cooker, bring up to pressure over medium-high heat; reduce heat enough to maintain steady pressure. Cook 10 minutes. Remove from heat.

For both models, let stand 15 minutes to release pressure naturally. Release any remaining pressure. Carefully open lid. Remove ramekins from pot. Cool on a wire rack 1 hour before serving. Or cool slightly, cover, and chill up to 6 hours. If chilled, let stand at room temperature 30 minutes before serving. Sprinkle with Cinnamon-Sugar Pepitas.

SLOW *1½-HOUR HIGH COOK TIME*

Pour 2 cups hot water into a 6-qt. oval slow cooker. Place ramekins in cooker. Cover and cook on high 1½ to 1¾ hours or until set. Remove ramekins from slow cooker. Let cool on a wire rack 1 hour before serving. Or cool slightly, cover, and chill up to 6 hours. If chilled, let stand at room temperature 30 minutes before serving. Sprinkle with Cinnamon-Sugar Pepitas.

CINNAMON-SUGAR PEPITAS

Preheat oven to 325°F. In a bowl combine ¼ cup raw pumpkin seeds (pepitas), 1½ tsp. melted butter, 1 tsp. sugar, and ¼ tsp. cinnamon; toss to coat. Spread in a 15×10-inch baking pan. Bake 15 to 18 minutes or until toasted, stirring occasionally.

PER SERVING *617 cal., 54 g fat (25 g sat. fat), 253 mg chol., 256 mg sodium, 27 g carb., 3 g fiber, 20 g sugars, 15 g pro.*

BLACK FOREST CHEESECAKE

[VEGETARIAN] [COMPANY]

Makes 6 servings

Nonstick cooking spray

¾ cup finely crushed chocolate graham crackers (10 squares)

1 Tbsp. sugar

2 Tbsp. butter, melted

12 oz. cream cheese, softened

½ cup sugar

1 Tbsp. all-purpose flour

½ tsp. vanilla

½ cup sour cream

3 eggs, lightly beaten

¼ cup snipped dried cherries

¼ cup miniature semisweet chocolate pieces

1 cup canned cherry pie filling

DIRECTIONS

Lightly coat a 6×3-inch springform pan with cooking spray. For crust, in a bowl stir together crushed crackers and the 1 Tbsp. sugar; stir in melted butter. Press onto bottom of the springform pan. Set aside. In a large bowl beat cream cheese with a mixer on medium 30 seconds. Beat in the ½ cup sugar, flour, and vanilla until combined. Beat in sour cream. Beat in eggs on low just until combined. Stir in dried cherries and 2 Tbsp. of the chocolate pieces. Pour over crust in pan. Prepare as directed for desired cooker, below.

FAST *35-MINUTE COOK TIME*

Place a steam rack in a 6-qt. electric or stove-top pressure cooker. Add 2 cups water to pot. To prevent crust from getting soggy while cooking, cut a piece of foil the size of a paper towel. Place foil under paper towel and set springform pan on paper towel; bring foil and paper towel up around the pan. From heavy foil cut three 18×3-inch foil strips; fold in half lengthwise. Crisscross strips and place pan on top of crisscross. Use foil strips to place pan on rack. Fold strips inside pot. Lock lid in place. Set an electric cooker on high to cook 35 minutes. For a stove-top cooker, bring up to pressure over medium-high heat; reduce heat enough to maintain steady pressure. Cook 35 minutes. Remove from heat.

For both models, let stand 15 minutes to release pressure naturally. Release any remaining pressure. Carefully open lid. Use foil strips to remove pan from cooker. Cool cheesecake on a wire rack 1 hour. Cover and chill 4 to 24 hours. Loosen and remove sides of pan. Top cheesecake with pie filling. Melt remaining 2 Tbsp. chocolate pieces and drizzle over cheesecake.

SLOW *2-HOUR COOK TIME*

Place a small rack in a 6-qt. slow cooker. Add warm water to cooker to just below rack. Set springform pan on rack. Cover opening of cooker completely with three layers of paper towels; place lid on top or cover with foil. Cook on high 2 hours. Turn off cooker and let stand, covered, 1 hour. Remove springform pan from cooker. Cool cheesecake on a wire rack 1 hour. Cover and chill 4 to 24 hours. Loosen and remove sides of pan. Top cheesecake with pie filling. Melt remaining 2 Tbsp. chocolate pieces and drizzle over cheesecake.

PER SERVING *559 cal., 33 g fat (18 g sat. fat), 170 mg chol., 325 mg sodium, 59 g carb., 1 g fiber, 44 g sugars, 9 g pro.*

DULCE DE LECHE CHEESECAKE

Makes 8 servings

- ¾ cup crushed vanilla wafers (about 21 wafers)
- 2 Tbsp. finely chopped toasted almonds (tip p. 20)
- 1 Tbsp. sugar
- 2 Tbsp. butter, melted
- 12 oz. cream cheese, softened
- ½ cup sugar
- 1 14-oz. can dulce de leche
- 3 eggs
- ½ tsp. pure vanilla extract
- 1 oz. bittersweet chocolate, melted

DIRECTIONS

Lightly coat a 6×3-inch springform pan with cooking spray. For crust, in a small bowl stir together crushed wafers, almonds, and the 1 Tbsp. sugar; stir in melted butter. Press onto bottom of the springform pan. In a large bowl beat cream cheese with a mixer on medium 30 seconds. Beat in the ½ cup sugar and ½ cup of the dulce de leche until combined. Beat in eggs on low just until combined. Beat in vanilla. Pour over crust in pan. Prepare as directed for desired cooker, below.

FAST   40-MINUTE COOK TIME

Place a steam rack in a 6-qt. electric or stove-top pressure cooker. Add 1 cup water to pot. To prevent crust from getting soggy while steaming, cut a piece foil the same size as a paper towel. Place foil under paper towel; set springform pan on paper towel; bring foil and paper towel up around pan.

Cut three double-thick, 18×3-inch heavy foil strips. Crisscross strips and place pan on top of crisscross. Use foil strips to place pan on rack. Fold strips inside pot. Lock lid in place. Set an electric cooker on high pressure to cook 40 minutes. For a stove-top cooker, bring up to pressure over medium-high heat; reduce heat enough to maintain steady pressure. Cook 40 minutes. Remove from heat.

For both models, let stand 15 minutes to release pressure naturally. Release any remaining pressure. Carefully open lid. Use foil strips to lift pan from cooker. Cool cheesecake on a wire rack 1 hour. Cover; chill 4 to 24 hours. Loosen and remove sides of pan; drizzle with remaining dulce de leche and chocolate.

SLOW   2-HOUR HIGH COOK TIME

Place a steam rack in a 6-qt. slow cooker. Add warm water to cooker to reach just below rack. Set springform pan on rack. Cover opening of cooker with three layers of paper towels; place lid on top. Cook on high 2 hours. Turn off cooker and let stand, covered, 1 hour. Remove springform pan from cooker. Cool cheesecake on a wire rack 1 hour. Cover; chill 4 to 24 hours. Loosen and remove sides from pan; drizzle cheesecake with remaining dulce de leche and chocolate.

PER SERVING 487 cal., 27 g fat (15 g sat. fat), 135 mg chol., 286 mg sodium, 52 g carb., 0 g fiber, 47 g sugars, 10 g pro.

INDEX

METRIC INFORMATION

PRODUCT DIFFERENCES

Most of the ingredients called for in the recipes in this book are available in most countries. However, some are known by different names. Here are some common American ingredients and their possible counterparts:

- Sugar (white) is granulated, fine granulated, or caster sugar.
- Powdered sugar is icing sugar.
- All-purpose flour is enriched bleached or unbleached white household flour. When self-rising flour is used in place of all-purpose flour in a recipe that calls for leavening, omit the leavening agent (baking soda or baking powder) and salt.
- Light-color corn syrup is golden syrup.
- Cornstarch is cornflour.
- Baking soda is bicarbonate of soda.
- Vanilla or vanilla extract is vanilla essence.
- Green, red, or yellow sweet peppers are capsicums or bell peppers.
- Golden raisins are sultanas.

VOLUME AND WEIGHT

The United States traditionally uses cup measures for liquid and solid ingredients. The chart (right) shows the approximate imperial and metric equivalents. If you are accustomed to weighing solid ingredients, the following approximate equivalents will be helpful.

- 1 cup butter, caster sugar, or rice = 8 ounces = ½ pound = 250 grams
- 1 cup flour = 4 ounces = ¼ pound = 125 grams
- 1 cup icing sugar = 5 ounces = 150 grams
- Canadian and U.S. volume for a cup measure is 8 fluid ounces (237 ml), but the standard metric equivalent is 250 ml.
- 1 British imperial cup is 10 fluid ounces.
- In Australia, 1 tablespoon equals 20 ml, and there are 4 teaspoons in the Australian tablespoon.
- Spoon measures are used for small amounts of ingredients. Although the size of the tablespoon varies slightly in different countries, for practical purposes and for recipes in this book, a straight substitution is all that's necessary. Measurements made using cups or spoons always should be level unless stated otherwise.

COMMON WEIGHT RANGE REPLACEMENTS

Imperial / U.S.	Metric
½ ounce	15 g
1 ounce	25 g or 30 g
4 ounces (¼ pound)	115 g or 125 g
8 ounces (½ pound)	225 g or 250 g
16 ounces (1 pound)	450 g or 500 g
1¼ pounds	625 g
1½ pounds	750 g
2 pounds or 2¼ pounds	1,000 g or 1 Kg

OVEN TEMPERATURE EQUIVALENTS

Fahrenheit Setting	Celsius Setting	Gas Setting
300°F	150°C	Gas Mark 2 (very low)
325°F	160°C	Gas Mark 3 (low)
350°F	180°C	Gas Mark 4 (moderate)
375°F	190°C	Gas Mark 5 (moderate)
400°F	200°C	Gas Mark 6 (hot)
425°F	220°C	Gas Mark 7 (hot)
450°F	230°C	Gas Mark 8 (very hot)
475°F	240°C	Gas Mark 9 (very hot)
500°F	260°C	Gas Mark 10 (extremely hot)
Broil	Broil	Grill

*Electric and gas ovens may be calibrated using Celsius. However, for an electric oven, increase Celsius setting 10 to 20 degrees when cooking above 160°C. For convection or forced-air ovens (gas or electric), lower the temperature setting 25°F/10°C when cooking at all heat levels.

BAKING PAN SIZES

Imperial / U.S.	Metric
9×1½-inch round cake pan	22- or 23×4-cm (1.5 L)
9×1½-inch pie plate	22- or 23×4-cm (1 L)
8×8×2-inch square cake pan	20×5-cm (2 L)
9×9×2-inch square cake pan	22- or 23×4.5-cm (2.5 L)
11×7×1½-inch baking pan	28×17×4-cm (2 L)
2-quart rectangular baking pan	30×19×4.5-cm (3 L)
13×9×2-inch baking pan	34×22×4.5-cm (3.5 L)
15×10×1-inch jelly roll pan	40×25×2-cm
9×5×3-inch loaf pan	23×13×8-cm (2 L)
2-quart casserole	2 L

U.S. / STANDARD METRIC EQUIVALENTS

⅛ teaspoon = 0.5 ml	
¼ teaspoon = 1 ml	
½ teaspoon = 2 ml	
1 teaspoon = 5 ml	
1 tablespoon = 15 ml	
2 tablespoons = 25 ml	
¼ cup = 2 fluid ounces = 50 ml	
⅓ cup = 3 fluid ounces = 75 ml	
½ cup = 4 fluid ounces = 125 ml	
⅔ cup = 5 fluid ounces = 150 ml	
¾ cup = 6 fluid ounces = 175 ml	
1 cup = 8 fluid ounces = 250 ml	
2 cups = 1 pint = 500 ml	
1 quart = 1 liter	